Being in the Pampas

The Question of Being in Argentine Literature

Julio César Díaz

Library of Congress Cataloging-in-Publication Data

Diaz, Julio Cesar.
Being in the pampas : the question of being in Argentine literature / Julio Cesar Diaz.
p. cm. -- (International studies in philosophy monograph series ; 2)
Includes bibliographical references.
ISBN-13: 978-1-58684-262-8 (alk. paper)
1. Ontology. 2. Spanish literature--Argentina. I. Title. II. Series.
BD301.D53 2005
199'.82--dc22
2005025761

Published by Global Academic Publishing
Binghamton University, LNG 99
Binghamton, New York 13902-6000 USA
Phone: (607) 777-4495. Fax: (607) 777-6132
E-mail: gap@binghamton.edu
Website: http://academicpublishing.binghamton.edu/

Contents

ACKNOWLEDGMENTS

In a gloomy afternoon of 1920, a man decided to lie down in the open. As he was staring at the vast extension of the land, he fell asleep, and dreamed. The images he saw, or imagined, did not quite belong to him—although he found them entirely familiar. He woke up suddenly, scared to death, and mumbled his recollections to his neighbors, who set him upon a chair and offered him some bread, but not before they heard his recollections. Those who listened to his story were less astonished by all its inconsistencies (a hare flying over the land), eccentricities (a coin that contained all the coins, but not all their values), and aimlessness (a man who killed another in order to become no one) than by its historical echoes.

As we may expect, time—which can only be measured in terms of motion—has handed down these recollections to us, but not without further additions, deletions, and emendations. Some say that the man dreamed of a captive woman; some others of a hare crossing the plain; a few of a lieutenant who dared to dig a wheel in order to unconceal truth in the pampas.... Most agree that the theme of his dream was, in any case, that of *Achilles*, Zeno's paradox.

As I was recollecting these stories in the winter of Binghamton, something compelled me to attempt to render Parmenides's verse, *τὸ γὰρ αὐτὸ νοεῖν ἔστιν τεχκαί εἶναι*, one more time, this one acknowledging the resemblance between its words and the dream of one, now of many. This may suffice to excuse the imperfections of this manuscript, not its thesis.

Borges used to say that frequently one is able to write a story, but not to understand its meaning. Perhaps the opposite is true as well, we may ponder upon its meaning, its inexhaustible, inscrutable meaning; but its precise form may evade us. I owe much of this book's thesis to Stephen David Ross, whose vast knowledge and unfailing encouragement have helped turn these recollections into a book. Kindness takes the simple form of a meal, or even the complex texture of a dream. Fulbright-Laspau has granted me both. My special thanks to Judith Adler (Fulbright-Laspau, U.S.A.), Carola Candurra (Fulbright-Laspau, U.S.A.), and Norma Gonzalez (Fulbright-Laspau, Argentina). A teaching assistantship from the PIC program at SUNY Binghamton has allowed me to present these ideas to the students who attended my lectures on images and philosophy during Spring 2001. Thanks as well to Dr. Yao, Chung-Kuen, chairperson of the Deparment of English Language and Literature, and to Dr. Tzai at the Language Center of Chinese Culture University, for showing a particular interest for this project even before it turned into a book. I have discussed these ideas with Iris Huang so many times that she can truly claim, *ξυνον δέ μοι εστιν* (Parmenides, Fragment 5).

J. C. D., Taipei, June 2004

The Question of Being

In the appendix to his *Lectures on the Philosophy of World History,* Hegel observes with respect to the self-unfolding of being that the natives of the *Río de la Plata* sleep continuously without stopping. So much so that they do not spend any time eating, discussing politics, or copulating. Indeed, the population dwindled so alarmingly that the Companion of Jesus was finally compelled to take extraordinary measures—such as ringing a bell every midnight in order to remind the aboriginals to perform their marital duties (Hegel, *Lectures on the Philosophy of World History,* 164–65).

Though Hegel's account is inaccurate geographically (e.g., the misleading name *Río de la Plata* instead of *Paraná*), we need to take seriously this remark on the very point of its inaccuracy—the inaccuracy that exceeds his telling—for what his account reveals is the significance, the weight of the *siesta* among the inhabitants of the pampas, as well as the way being unfolds itself there through the activity of *siesta, ἡσυχία.*

Is it not astonishing, then, that about two centuries after this first glimpse, the question of being in the pampas appeared in Macedonio's methodical *siesta*? Borges himself reports in a bold and emotional statement that "one afternoon in a back patio on Sarandí Street he told us that if he were able to go to the country and stretch out on the ground at midday and close his eyes and understand, divesting his mind of circumstances that distract us, he would be able to resolve immediately the enigma of the universe. I do not know if that blessing was granted him, but he undoubtedly glimpsed it" (Borges, *Autobiographical Essay*, 77; Cf. Fernández, *Macedonio: Selected Writings in Translation*, 110).

In any inquiry or investigation there are steps to be followed. In the pampas there are paths, hoofprints, stories, and images. Not only must one enclose the subject of inquiry, but also the activity to which that inquiry belongs. Next one must ensure that one is "mature enough" to pursue the questions posed. In this sense the question of being in the pampas is a shameful one: when the question of being arises in the pampas, the philosopher raising the question risks being seen as a perpetual child who needs to learn under the strictest discipline and chastisement. A child who still needs to "go to school and for a long time" before beginning to philosophize. Besides, how can we claim to solve the question of being, which belongs to the realm of activity and motion, by reaching stillness?* Isn't it an untransversable contradiction, a regress *ad infinitum*, to solve a problem that requires the convulsion of the body by reaching stillness, the major *inactivity*?

Furthermore, there are those who claim that any account of being in the pampas should deal with alteration, depreciation, and devaluation, but without detaching itself from that primordial stillness, the one that "gives laws." Like the Huiliche Indians, (Cf. Aira, *The Hare*, 27) who persist in replying that the question of being in the pampas is easy to answer for it is enough to open our eyes, look at the many images, and hear the many words—the continuum itself. Being in the pampas is, then, to be thought in terms of default, of the hyperinflation of being, for alteration is in the realm of coming to be and passing away.** The question that is more difficult to pursue, they say, is one of the discontinuity of the territory, for that question must be answered in terms of an infinite regress.

It has been pointed out, however, that finding any answer to the question of being in the pampas has to begin by following its many paths, hoofprints, rumors, stories, and images. The task of ontology becomes, then, one of reporting (*ἱστορεῖν*), "being there"—a doll hanging on a rancho's wall, a man riding to his death in a carriage, a proud and timid boy from the outskirts, the echoes of "*razza di cani!*"* carried by the wind, the dream of one. All of these situate the inquiry in the continuum in such a way that the question exceeds its bounds to become many questions. It is by following these many paths that we may answer what it is to render the question of being in the pampas, by following images and signs *ad infinitum.*

There are some who compare ontology with photography, for both activities concern themselves with images: the task of rendering *εἶναι* and that of taking photos are one and the same from the standpoint of the One.** But they reject alteration as a ground for incongruence, and go on to propose montage, the framework, as a shift from the pampas, the mere cow, to technology.

Besides, there is a rumor saying that being in the pampas is the consequence of centuries of muddying being, which both takes and exceeds any place, with the category of *place* itself, which answers the question *ποῦ*. Clearly, these are two questions. Only our promiscuous characters, the Huiliches, have mixed them up into one. Any attempt to locate Parmenides in the pampas is doomed to fail, for one must provide an account of the many paths that follow the question of being. Such an attempt could only be a fallacious anachronism, for how could Parmenides still be living in the pampas after all these centuries? Is he *de juris* an Argentinean citizen?

To a certain extent these views are granted by, or rely on, temporality. If one is to find a continuous answer to the question of being in the pampas, one needs to show that the question is primordially one of *place;* that any attempt to reduce the question of being to a strictly temporal understanding will hide the convulsions of the bodies, the sudden revolts, the gossip, depreciations, atrocious crimes, and superhuman devotions that ontology unavoidably includes. Thus, it is by means of these detours, whimsical assertions, regresses *ad infinitum,* insolences, and the many paths and muddy hoofprints that we may reach our achievement.

It is said that the question of being in the pampas, if indeed it is possible to conceive this question, must not be different from the question of being in general. When the Eleatic thinkers raised this question, for instance, they did not approach it as a question of "local colors," or of "frivolous nationalism," but as an inquiry on the notes that being may echo, on the many ways that being may manifest itself. The history of ontology is the collection of those tenets. Doxography has separated these from the biographies, and has unified them in a corpus, thematized them, and arranged them into a tentative historical path of thinking called Western thought. Only an act of some perverse cruelty, of childish whim, could posit the question of being otherwise. And what kind of answer are we supposed to get from such a *κόρος*, from such insolence? The question of being in the pampas should, at most, be a question bounded, circumscribed by the rendering of *εἶναι* into the Spanish language, an inquiry into the very feasibility of doing a translation of the pre-Socratic works into Argentinean Spanish.

We must first inquire about this way of doing ontology, of refusing to ask what it means to be without also asking *where*. How is this task to be carried out when within such a translation is hidden an entire range of questions and problems that arise when one begins reading the Eleatic fragments into the vast geography of the pampas, and when it is only some cruelty on our part that enables us to unfold the question of being there, since such an account always necessarily leaves aside the numerous other echoes, voices, interpretations that a text may also have?* Such an act of cruelty is the condition for unfolding the bodies, for doubling the gestures, and for exhibiting what has become of being in the pampas: depreciation, the dream of many, the captive, a hare, mintage, fashion, the murderous events of New Rome, the bureaucracy of being.** Further, if being unfolded itself in many ways through the territory, to the point that it unfolded itself to become its many paths, we must explain the relation between these hoofprints and the politics behind the continuum, for in the Huiliche tongue "path" also means "government" or "hare." That is, "path" already includes in its definition the notion of the inflation of being, its inexhaustibility, its twists and turns, its lavishness, its excess. Our view does not differ from that of those who claim that there is a continuum between the notion of being and that of being in the pampas. Yet their procedure is wholly unsatisfactory, for unless there is alteration, depreciation, devaluation, and cruel exchange rates, no answer may exhibit being in the pampas as mintage, representation, fashion show. Without alteration, the task of following an answer's path becomes unbearable.

This is why some have defined metaphysics as "a branch of fictional literature,"* for ontology appears to them to posit conjectural order in the middle of chaos. This dwelling in literature allows the thematization of uncertainty as fully present in being by lying still and by reaching motion. This is the case with Macedonio Fernández, who vislumbrated that being can be exhibited by means of *siesta*. His "making up" the answer that must be given pointed out that the question we are touching upon is not just any other question, in other words, that we do not ask only about the meaning of *being* in the pampas. We inquire how being placed itself in the pampas, how being became a continuum in the pampas, even became the pampas itself. We ask under what depreciation cycle did being become coming-to-be and passing away—taxable, lawless, familiar.

In asking this question we are detaching ourselves from a traditional view of ontology—a view that claims that the question of being should be thought primarily in terms of *time*, before and after. Instead, we are raising the question of being in terms of *place*, here and there. In doing so, we follow what was said by the Eleatic philosophers, (Cf. Parmenides, Fragment 5–7) who, in their perceptive understanding of being, not only acknowledged *place* and *void* as the notions that guided them toward truth, but also displayed truth in a continuum of voices, sounds, images, and rumors that created a path toward the question of being in the pampas. They showed that the One always exceeds itself, represents itself, and spreads itself here and there and always beyond Velia. This is revealed in the taking place of being in Laodicea, Cesarea, Rhodes, Alexandria, Numidia, and Syria. And wasn't this ontology? Did it perish at all?

This outburst, this radical motion, this dissemination of being provided a stimulus for the research of Plato, Aristotle, Galen, Simplicius, and Diogenes Laertius. All of them attempted to preserve the many fragments of the Eleatic school in a continuum. What was achieved in these centuries was to persist through many alterations, retellings, emendations, glosses, and "retouchings" down to Hudson's description of the pampas, the murderous events of New Rome, Borges's analysis of the Argentinean adjectives, and *ἡσυχία*, the intellectual efforts of the *siesta*.

Thus, Parmenides' presentation of being makes it possible for us to raise the question of being in the pampas. Parmenides' poem is a doctrine dictated by a goddess without a name, a goddess who revealed the scandalous thesis that everything is One (Cf. Heidegger, *Parmenides*, 1–16). She said we *ού γὰρ ἀποτμήξει τό ἐὸν τοῦ ἐόντος ἔχεσθαι*, "should not cut off what is in being from holding fast to what is in being" (Parmenides, Fragment 4), but this is an imperative that the history of ontology risks leaving behind when it attempts to construct a chronological account of being that claims universality by becoming the emptiest of concepts (Cf. Heidegger, *Being and Time*, 21–23)—a concept that has severed what is in being from that which is in being by asking what it means to be without also asking where.

Those, then, who say there is no need to raise the question of being in the pampas since it is no different from the question of being in general are making a mistake, forget that being there is not necessarily the same as being here, that the Huiliches are not Parmenides is not the hare is not the goddess is not Macedonio is not New Rome.

Until now, the question of being in the pampas has been set aside in the philosophical circles of Buenos Aires in the fear that historically there is no such need, that "we are not ready yet," that the notion of being has already been interpreted elsewhere, or that it must remain implied in our many gestures. But once we posit the problem of being in chronological terms, before and after, we show a lack of continuity, sever being from place, something that the ancient thinkers might have looked upon with astonishment or concern, for we have taken as self-evident what they found most disturbing, obscure, and hidden. We may note that what compelled them to preserve fragments, to comment upon them, to add biography, and to refer to the place where a thinker was born, was to give a truthful account of that which was taking place there rather than what is taking place here. That is the reason why they did not hesitate to offer precise accounts of customs, habits, and prejudices that are to be constantly kept and reimplanted, acknowledging the many voices, retellings, and echoes coming out of ancient ontology. If we are to give an answer to the question of being in the pampas we need to restate this chorus.

Besides, the question of being in the pampas is already placed in many paradoxes that cause disquietude. These paradoxes are located in Argentine's literature as conundrums, as echoes and retellings that censor, circulate, and distort the many voices, and themselves show that the question of being in the pampas is a question of *place, void, stillness, motion,* and regress *ad infinitum.* They detach us from any account of being bound within strictly temporal terms.

1. With regard to the mintage of coins, and the many cycles of depreciation and devaluation, one of the schools declares, "If there is a plurality of coins, these must be as many as they are. No more and no less"; and then, "If there is a plurality of coins, the coins in circulation are uncountable; for there will always be other coins between those that are, and yet others between those others. And so the things that are, are uncountable." Some understand this as a skeptical account, whose main political goal is to leave aside the *convertibilidad*—to replace Argentina's peg exchange rate by a bewildering exchange rate system. But this rumor is meant to exhibit the hyper-inflationary character of *εἶναι,* which *ser* does not quite exhibit (i.e., that any plurality is to exceed itself). Aira reports how under this dogmatic assumption, the Indians organized an aesthetic revolt by means of which individuals might be entitled to mint their own coins (Cf. Aira, *Ema, la Cautiva,* 169–72).

2. A second argument concerning motion causes disquietudes, blackmailing, and frequent suicides among the line troops installed at the frontier. It is also said that Darwin himself fell victim to it twice.* In *Fuerte Argentino* some spread rumors saying, "It is manifest by its visible effects, that in the plains a traveler never quite arrives at his destiny, for 'before one can reach the far end one must first reach the half-way point; but before one reaches the half-way point one must reach a point half-way to it; and so on ad infinitum.'" There are some who observed that Olivieri's murder might be related to the fact that he avoided this conundrum by traveling by sea. Others focus on a moral conclusion that is not understood yet. It is well known that some use the notion of *ἄπειρον* to solve the very same conundrum, by saying that the traveler reached the end *by exceeding his own motion,* not unusual when one has a good horse. The obscene or monstrous implication is that being—whether at rest or in motion—exceeds its own place. They inferred it from the passage in which Plato asks, *Οὕτω δὴ πεφυκὸς τὸ ἕν ἆρ᾽ οὐκ ἀνάγκη καὶ κινεῖσθαι καὶ ἑστάναι;* Plato, *Parmenides,* 145e).

3. Perhaps the most notorious of these misleading hoofprints is "the captive," for we find ourselves in trouble when we try to explain

how the chieftain captured the white woman. Some reason that in a *malón* the quickest chieftain never seizes the white woman, since the Indian must first reach the point whence the poor woman started, so that the slow woman must always hold a lead. In this case, it follows that the chieftain could never catch the captive. Women, naturally, tend to reject this argument adducing the fact that all human beings partake of *speed*. But any participation in Platonic ideas is far from being settled. Old women, wisely, claim that there is no reason to believe that the captive herself ran more than half of her own distance, and eventually the chieftain overtook her. But, if that were the case, how are we to explain the many transformations that the captive suffered, to become a blue-eyed boy lost in Junin, or a blue-eyed English woman? This is the reason why some adopted the idealism of Berkeley within which being and its temporal images are linked by pure association. It is said that Olivieri preferred to solve the paradox by means of three Greek notions that sent him to his doom, *κόρος* (satiety, insolence, surfeit, the fattiness of being), *ὑπερέχον* (to rise above oneself, excess), *πόρος* (pathways, taxable estate), and ξυνός (that which is familiar, common, continuous). Even though the translation of these terms is under censorship, it is said, for instance, that the chieftain eventually realized the difficulty, and he exceeded his own place, so quickly did he run. This is granted by the continuum, which the Huiliches explain by a hare running in such a way that for any discussion on the captive, in the exposition of this perplexing problem, faith is not necessary. Whenever one travels one perceives such an excess in hares, Indians, captives, and women in general. Indeed, one may notice that such a path avoids any inquiries concerning the political-hygienic as such, just as everyone understands that "the hare took off, vanished, or was stolen" (Cf. Aira, *The Hare,* 39). And it is claimed that this is only an average kind of intelligibility. Coliqueo, for instance, within the range of his philosophic-hygienic concept of pampas, does not invoke any self evidence except that of the phenomena, which are always self evident in their richness as processes of mintage and depreciation (Cf. Aira, *The Hare,* 127). There is, however, the implicit recognition, if not the open celebration of these changes without which the reality of the continuum could be unbearable. It is from there that we must first work out an adequate way of formulating the question of being in the pampas.

4. After the bloody *malón* of April 11th 1869, another paradox was known in *Fuerte Argentino.* It says, "An object is at rest when it occupies a place equal to itself.* An arrow in flight occupies, at any given moment, a space equal to itself. Therefore, an arrow in flight is at rest." At dawn you could still hear the noisy, bitter discussion of it coming from the fortress. Soldiers, some perhaps acquainted with the philosophical literature dealing with the arrow, assumed that the Indians, as well as their predecessor Zeno, were skeptics with regard to motion. But the *malón* proved that such an account is only the product of a reductive ontology. The only solution to the political problem of the discontinuity of territory is to assume that *beings exceed their own place,* a compromising solution that may exceed itself as well.

Κόρος

The paradoxes manifest the question of being in the pampas. As hoofprints, they do not lead toward skepticism, to a manifest denial of motion, or the unreality of time. Following them along zig-zagging paths, the continuum is taken for granted, but not merely temporally. The same phenomenon is exhibited by images, sounds, signs, coins, and clothes. These are by no means linked *by* time or *in* time, unless by time we understand ek-static time, the excess of that which has already been there. They do not walk along the path taken by historicizing ontology, which claims that images and signs are limited, bound, taking only their own place in a certain time. The paradoxes show that the question of being in the pampas is not a problem of the temporal linkage between images or signs, but of displaying being in terms that "neither disperse themselves in every way everywhere, nor gather themselves together" (Cf. Parmenides, Fragment 4). Historicizing ontology leads us to seek for the time in which such and such image or sign has been developed or acquired. Equally, chronology places the captive in a provisional continuum made of "times" that configures her being as a manifestation of some atemporal unfolding, in many versions that take their place in time (Cf. Dopchie, "À Propos de *Koros* dans l'Agamemnon d'Eschyle: Mise au Point Préliminaire." *Recherches de Philologie et de Linguistique* (1968): 125–138).

In asking the question of being in the pampas, we are moving along paths and following hoofprints heading toward a particular direction, that of the paradoxes which make manifest the question of being as a question of *place*. It is for this reason that the Huiliche Indians insist on postulating that being may exceed itself in giving an account of motion and rest in the pampas. For instance, one travels because one has already traveled, and vice-versa. Thus, "what is so hidden that it is necessary to travel the globe to find it, but at the same time is so visible that it can be found simply by going to look for it? By definition such a thing must be anywhere and everywhere, wherever one may be ..." (Aira, *The Hare*, 22). Here, *anywhere* does not have the connotation that has so often suppressed notions of place from the history of ontology, but concernfully denotes that things tend to exceed themselves; and this is what is acknowledged, displayed by the term *κόρος*.

Κόρος, it is objected, is a term borrowed from Greek poetry. Fearing that they may bore their audience with their recitals, poets keep them within temporal boundaries. A bored audience could become insolent, distracted, or violent. Traditional temporal ontology interprets *κόρος* as a concern with regard to time. But such an account of *κόρος* seems correct only if we are to lay bare the notion of *time* in ontology by terms that exceed time itself, for *κόρος* is related primarily and foremost to "making space," and with "making room in one's stomach for more food." Greek thinkers knew that excessive food produces drowsiness, satiety, and in the end, insolence. This last sense is unfolded by Pindar's *Olympian Ode I*, where the poet describes how the insatiable Tantalos couldn't digest his happiness, ambrosia, *ἀλλά γὰρ καταπέψαι/ μέγαν ὄλβον οὐκ ἐδυνάσθη, κόρῳ δ' ἕλεν/ ἄταν ὑπέροπλον*, "He [Tantalos] could not digest his great bliss *[ὄλβιος]*, and with his insatiability *[κόρος]*, he brought upon himself an overwhelming disaster *[ἄτε]?*" (Pindar, *Olympian Odes*, I, 55–57; Cf. Nagy, *Pindar's Homer*, 131). It does not have much of a theoretical nature, but it has to do with a politic-hygienic issue: How much fire is an excess for the stomach? In ontology, how could we forget food and drink? (Cf. Homer, *Iliad*, XIX, 231; XXIV, 601).

Κόρος, then, displays this "making room" as a conundrum: How can bodies take more place than themselves? How can place take more place than itself? The Pythagoreans, Plato, Plotinus, and Origen all thought of *κόρος* as an image of falling souls in terms of making room, of this excess of place. In contemplating the divine, psyches *exceed* their own "capacity" for contemplation (Cf. Harl, "Recherches sur l'origenisme d'Origene: la 'Satiété' (*Koros*) de la Contemplation comme Motif de la Chute des Âmes." *Studia Patristica*, VIII, (1966), 373–405. Such an excess must be punished by means of embodiment, by means of giving some defined, perhaps more restrained body.

Yet, through their contortions, their hexameters, and their many gestures, poets also caused *κόρος*. Traditional philosophy has thematized this excess, this surfeit of being, in terms of time. This approach, for example, is manifest in Aristotle's *Poetics* and its concern for the length of a tragedy, for the *ὁ δὲ κατ᾽ αὐτὴν τὴν φύσιν τοῦ πράγματος ὅρος*, for the natural limit of actions that may exhibit something that goes beyond actions (Cf. *Poetics*, 1451a10–12). On the contrary, in the language of the Huiliche everything tends toward *κόρος*, but of course they do not use Greek for dealing with the political problems of the discontinuity of the territory, motion, and rest. Are this standing still, this *siesta* after a fest, and this violent series of insolent contortions precisely what are required for answering the question of being in the pampas?

We are acquainted with chronicles, supernatural stories, retellings of gossip on trifle matters, cruel images, hocus-pocus, and Greek fragments as taking place in the pampas. Anyone initiated in the mysteries of *κόρος* should learn from such trivia. Indeed, it is said that these are not, strictly speaking, part of philosophy. These are, so to speak, the grease, the residue, the surplus that needs to be filtered out from a chronology of fragments.

In our thematizing of the question of being in the pampas, we are to move away from any strictly temporal notion of *κόρος*. Our journey should lead toward the display, toward the exhibition of the ways in which being has unfolded itself there. We are to celebrate that *κόρος*, that excess, and that insolence, for these are the very condition of being in the territory. This was also our objective in positing Parmenides in the pampas: to evince how being takes place, how being can exceed its own place, and proliferate, circulate, wander, and dwell in different places. Our insistence on the fact that this should be a journey toward the South was not completely arbitrary, but a sign that makes manifest, that displays the hollow, inexhaustible character of *ser*. In the Spanish language, as spoken in the pampas, being seems to resist this kind of gratuitous expression. Chronology reports all sorts of gender troubles, impersonal forms, and cultisms taking place in the pampas. At a certain time in the 17th century, an *adelantado* still found it fashionable to say *"la isla de Santa Catalina que es entre San Vicente y el Río de la Plata"*—the island of St. Cataline which *is* between San Vicente and the Río de la Plata—as well as *"soy obligado"*—I am forced to—but such expressions disappeared in the turmoil, to become obsolete under depreciation (Cf. Fontanella de Weinberg, *Aspectos del Español Hablado en el Río de la Plata durante los Siglos XVI y XVII*, 33). Since then, perhaps the opinion that being in the pampas should not be thematized in terms of *place* but only in terms of *time* has become hegemonic. The question of being in the pampas, then, has been taken as a mockery, as an ill product of thinking being. In thinking the question of *ser*, we barely acknowledge that we are doing so from the pampas, and that being may disclose itself here too. The question about the meaning of being in the pampas is to be formulated in such a way that it displays an excessive continuum of being.

This task is made plain in literature, for literature exhibits what is marginal, what has been pushed out of the frontiers of philosophy (Cf. Derrida, *Marginis of Philosophy*, ix–xxix; Kusch, "La Seducción de la Barbarie," in Kuch, *Obras Completas*, 3–131). It is repeatedly said that everything that could not be said or formulated in philosophy was ventured in literature, and with a manifest excess that took over the place of philosophy itself with regard to ontology. Eventually, the rejected question of being in the pampas came back as the theme by itself, as the traces unfolding the way being displayed itself in the pampas. Hudson, for instance, observed that in dealing with metaphysics, the gauchos always preferred to convey it through their stories, ballads, and rather whimsical compositions, for these were more expressive, vivid. Hudson preferred it this way himself. His *Purple Land* is less a story of an Englishman traveling through the *cuchillas* of Uruguay, than a report on his own transformation: a case of mimesis, of becoming-gaucho, of being otherwise.

Anyone acquainted with his *Purple Land* may notice that Hudson avoids inquiring about being in the pampas by giving a chronology of endless wars between *Blancos* and *Colorados*. He addresses the question of being in the pampas by displaying the murder, the exile, the put-on, the frustration of being-there. He also made manifest the mimesis taking place in his body while dealing with trifling matters, in his final bewildering collapse, and in his forced—and yet truthful return—to England. He shows that being in the pampas is already manifest to us (i.e., as a proliferation of rumors, endless stories, retellings, gossip, Greek mythology, and the dream of one). There is, however, a certain indefiniteness in the way that being makes itself manifest: its fondness for dwelling in fragments, its leaning toward gossip and apocryphal biographies, its needy reliance on the contradictory accounts given by travelers, obsessions, and images that haunt the gauchos. These testimonies, these tenets make explicit the meaning of both the pampas and being as exceeding their place, as *ἄπειρον*.

We have pointed out that in their perceptive understanding the Huiliche Indians acknowledge and welcome the fact that being in the pampas is always subject to alteration, hyperinflation, exaggerations of any sort—manifest or hidden under a certain nostalgia for the past, an unexpected visit, detailed answers to that which belongs to mere curiosity, or any compliment. There are also some other accounts of the *κόρος* kept in traveler's journals such as those written by Darwin, Hegel, and Hudson.

The question of being in the pampas lets us see that *ser* is not only a hollow verb, a verb that after centuries has lost its power to denote state or place. Even if *ser* has been deprived of these functions, it does not preclude us from giving an account of being, for the question of being in the pampas has been preceded by certain interpretations of early Greek thinkers. In addressing the question of being in the pampas, we are following a path traced by a preliminary work on Parmenides in the pampas. That attempt anticipated many of the conclusions of the present study. Its fragmentary character, its many repetitions, its acknowledgement of alteration and the cycles of depreciation, its emphasis on the need for cruelty, its suggestion that the goddess without name displayed images to Parmenides, all of these signs attempted to exhibit how being itself took place in the pampas.

Parmenides claimed that everything is One, but how can a territory, such as the pampas, that is in itself discontinuous, be One? How can someone dare to postulate that the cycles of depreciation themselves (and not something beneath these) are One? How can it be said that the laugh, the excess, the shortage of currency, the starvation of many, and a theater play are One? How can it be claimed that the One is in the pampas twisted, mingled, mixed, hyperinflated, represented, in and by images? Was that work a product of *κόρος*? Did it really reveal that being always exceeds itself? Wasn't it preceded by a reading, a certain interpretation of Parmenides' poem; by an *Auslegung* that could grant such a displacement from Velia toward the pampas?

Parmenides in the pampas was preceded by a provisional rendering of *εἶναι* as "what is in being," instead of "what exists," or "what is present" as suggested by temporality. We were carried by a goddess who claimed that everything is in being, and that everything in the pampas is also in being. The goddess herself showed, displayed, exhibited the many images of what is in being. She said ... *τὸ γὰρ αὐτὸ νοεῖν ἔστιν τε καί εἶναι*—"it is the same what you see with your eyẹs and what is in being" (Parmenides, Fragment 3) and in the next four fragments the goddess herself displayed many images, under the imperative *οὐ γὰρ ἀποτμήξει τὸ ἐόν τοῦ ἐόντος ἔχεσθαι*, "you should not cut off what is in being from holding fast to what is in being" (Parmenides, Fragment 4). Manifestly, the goddess herself exceeded the boundaries of her own speech in her will to show what is in being. In her speech, she is addressing unfaithful truth (*ἀλήθεια*), but also being, death, sex, reproduction, naming practices, shades, fashion, astronomy; and indeed, in a way that made manifest that *ξυνὸν δέ μοί ἐστιν*, that everything is familiar to her (Parmenides, Fragment 5). Yet, there are questions which we have passed by in silence. Did the unnamable goddess laugh, recite, order, demand, request, or advice? Is she also in debt? Indebted?

Such an attempt was brief in scope and interrupted by the many cycles of depreciation, vituperated and almost completely forgotten. Yet, it showed that being is boundless, limitless, *ἄπειρον*. The Spanish language exhibits this *ἄπειρον* character. The expression "to tell a story" makes manifest a tendency toward a regress *ad infinitum*. Argentineans literally say "to count a story" in a way that does not refer to clear cut stories and numbers. A story itself is to be "recounted" by adding monstrous or obscene details; this is the very definition of censorship in the pampas. Some also suggest "to count a history" instead of the spurious form "story." It is in this counting of (hi)stories that one may find a disclosure of being in the pampas.

A strictly temporal understanding commits the error of reducing these stories to a mere having been (*Die Vergangenheit*), a trifling rumor of the *they*. We call such an account *doxographic*, for it primarily deals with the chronology of what has been said. Such an account avoids depictions of being that have to do with *place:* mere anecdotes full of local flavors, inventions, lies. When we suggest that this has been the history of ontology, that being has been thematized in that way, as collections of doctrines, rumors, *apocryphal* biographies, anecdotes, opinions, as addressing the question of what was taking place in other towns and what was taking place here; we are accused of irrationality, or of falling back into a time when men expressed thinkers' views quite fragmentarily, and in often colored or biased ways. Doxography, it is said, is topic oriented, and addresses two issues with regard to being: the faithful account of what a philosopher's views are, and the sources of these tenets. Only when you deviate from this division are you then able to inquire about being in the pampas. Only then can you allude to a situation that hares, Indians, travelers, gauchos, and women equally endure. *Dasein* itself turns out to be *in* what is to be interrogated. Thus, such a zigzagging detour is not considered thinking and does not have anything to do with thinking itself.

From the standpoint of the history of philosophy, however, being in the pampas is a redundant or manifestly ill-grounded question. Being takes place in the pampas as in any other place. *Place* itself is irrelevant, untaxable. Motion, the reception of fragments and images, is no other thing than motion *in time* according to a measure between before and after that moves away from repetition. Philosophy does not take place in the pampas for the simple reason that there have not been philosophers there *yet*. Accordingly, before inquiring about being in the pampas it is necessary to undertake a certain philosophical anthropology that may describe the "character" of its inhabitants. From such a description one may infer what is reasonable to expect from them, namely their disclosures of being. To depict the Huiliches, then, is to portray them in terms of their virtues and foibles, but such an analysis risks forgetting the convulsions, the contortions of the body, the inner cruelty of the gauchos, the rage of the captive, the incongruencies of almost everyone there, as well as everything that points out certain doubling of the bodies. Any future philosopher must have those notes. There are, also, individuals who are already left behind: dogs and illegitimate children for example. Borges himself believed that being could not be clearly manifested in Kika de González Achaval. What is there to say about cows, hares, or the captive herself? Is our starting point provisional, theatrical so to speak? Should we take into account Laralde's testimony? (Hudson, *The Purple Land*, 244–248). Which entity shall we take as a specimen, and in what sense does it have priority? Who can not claim to be *Dasein* there?*

We are to ask the question of being in the pampas in such a way that it makes manifest, exhibits, displays how being is taking place in the pampas and vice versa. To ensure that we are able to carry out this task we need to address the question of being in the pampas that elucidates the role of *place, motion,* and *rest* in shaping the question itself. In doing so we are to engage ourselves in the task of showing that the way the history of ontology has been carried out concealed the question of *place* beneath the veil of time; that any such a question about time and being makes manifest its limits, for it bounds entities to be what they actually are, to keep their place, and to never exceed their place.

It may be objected that we are falling into a manifest regress *ad infinitum* in postulating that being exceeds itself, that such an account grounded on *place* already erases distinctions that for centuries philosophers have made between philosophy and poetry, between truth and stories, between philosophical tenets and mere anecdotes, between the philosophical dialogue and the theater, between allegorical uses of images, and images themselves. Moreover, such a regress *ad infinitum* has already taken place in a temporal account of being, for in its having been there, in the pampas, time is already exceeding itself. Haven't thinkers already revealed that signs are always displacing, deferring, and disseminating their meaning? Weren't they already engaging themselves in a criticism of the history of ontology? Isn't it manifest in the *destruktion* of the history of ontology, in the return to the pre-Socratic thinkers? Didn't we adopt the notion of truth as *ἀλήθεια,* which already comes from the Eleatic school? Why should we engage ourselves in such an attempt that already showed its scopes and limits? What can philosophy profit from such a practice?

Accordingly, we are to address Greek thinkers as a whole, as a community debating on being *qua* being in time. One may cast doubts on such an interpretation and observe that the pre-Socratic philosophers came from different places, that they were full of rivalry, suspicion, and wonder toward each other. One may also observe that it is only because of a certain historical kindness that we see all of them as Greek. For these thinkers, indeed, the question of place was primordial rather than foundational. They barely attempted a temporal account of being, for what mattered was what took place in other towns and what could take place there. This is apparent in their interest in biographical information, anecdotes and stories. Such a dissemination took place not because of *time* but because of wonder, because of their desire for knowledge, for gossiping about what was taking place in another place. Any such account invariably began with a life of the philosopher—not as mere addition or censorship, but out of genuine interest in knowing how being had displayed itself hither and yon.

Hexameter smoothed the way for the circulation and the alteration of being: in its taking place, being was to be spread, distorted, corrected, added, deleted, and forgotten. In any case, we are not seeking a *destruktion* of the history of philosophy, but unbounding it from the conception of *time* understood as before and after, a conception that deprives it of voices, images, recollections. We are also moving away from a certain way of thinking that took too much care in separating verbatim fragments from the *testimonia*, that manifested itself in an effort to arrange the fragments according to a *succession*, in such a way that the chronological order split the fragments away from their sources, and in doing so, separated the opinion of a thinker from the account given in another place, but forgetting that any distortion from the original was also the source of a proliferation of ontology into other places.

What awaits us, then, is the acknowledgment that being in the pampas unfolds itself in endless discussions, gossipings, misunderstandings, fragmentation, rivalry between many schools continuously adding, deleting, copying, forgetting being. In doing so, we keep the goddess's precept "you should not cut off what is in being from holding fast to what is in being," a precept that we have already understood as the continuum between places.

At Delphi

Once again I am walking through that path. A path that was already there, before the questions, before Persephone, even before the Libertador and his silver body. I am crossing the crab shallows, beating my chest and tearing my clothes apart, but without asking about εἶναι. About how I translated εἶναι. As if a verb, this ancient and hollow verb, could settle the meaning of an erratic translation.

I had the translation in mind before I arrived in Bahía to work as a substitute teacher, but not all its images. To get them, I simply let my limbs cross the muddy path, and rest in a yellow room.

I lay in bed and I rested until very late in the afternoon.

My first recollections of the town are nocturnal. A bed in a room painted yellow. A room without windows. A guest house near the train station. Then, Soler street. My eyes are widely opened, and I am trying to recollect the time when I came to Bahía Blanca before the conflagration. One becomes a teacher because one has already been one. I lay still, and for days I did not know of any other pleasure.

In my childhood I used to lie still. It was far more than a pastime, it was an activity. Ησυχία. *I lay on the floor, or in bed. With my eyes widely opened, to the point that they were almost completely dry. And then, when I couldn't stand the glowness any more, I closed them, and I tried to recollect the many forms I saw on the wall. I was able to recall at once more than eleven forms. Some of them were imaginary forms, a mixture of columns and shields, or of faces and bricks. They were present in the room. And they devoured my eyes* (Cf. Kingsley, *In the Dark Places of Wisdom;* Pausanias, *Description of Greece,* II, 348–355).

Free of memory and hope, alteration offers its cycles of oblivion (Cf. Derrida, *Margins of Philosophy,* 31–67; Saussure, *Course in General Linguistics,*

173–176). *Conflagration lets one live several lives in one life. As many as one can have, or even dream of. Partial lives. Incomplete, occasional, absurd, brief, colorful lives. Cycles.*

In the vase, all the images moved (Cf. Trendall, *Red Figure Vases of South Italy and Siciliy*, 151–210).

That is the camera that I bought in a pawn-house. In Soler street, a block from the train station. A camera with a silver body.

*She, breastless. "She … ," a Libertador, fulfilled and impossible, leading the way to a vast, immense universe summarized in the womb of a cave.**

I spent the following afternoon window shopping. Distracted. Careless. At that time it still pleased me to see my face and my body reflected on the glass of a shop-window. A manly face in a childish, troubled body. What a foolish game! It was right behind my body figure, over my left shoulder, where I saw the camera. In the reflected image, it appeared next to a guitar and a bronze bedstead. I look at myself one more time before walking into the shop. Inside, I looked around, but I didn't stare at the camera. I browsed for a marble figure, for a table lamp. I asked for the price of every item at the window, and bargained over their prices. While the attention of the owner was focused on the lamp, mine was far aside—behind his back, through the window, across the street, where there was a man standing with a camera. I suddenly went off, and I approached the man. He offered me the camera for a cigarette or two, but I treated him to dinner, for he came from behind the mountains.

With my silver body, I may turn all the forms into light and dark night (Cf. Parmenides, Fragments 8 and 9).

A procession of feminine goddesses. The goddess without name. The one called δαίμονος, *at the beginning of the poem. The* Ἡλιάδες κοῦραι, *Daughters of the Sun.* Μοῖρα. Δίκη. Θέμις. *Even the horses. All of them are feminine figures, figures whose shadows I saw many times on a wall* (Cf. Parmenides, Fragments 1–3, 14, 16).

Parmenides' poem relies upon many demonstratives: he mèn, he dè, tèn dé…. Including einai. They are pointing beyond the poem. Toward an image. Toward an absent image, "There, the gates of the journey of Night and Day" (Fragment 1, 11), "That I declare to be a path entirely unlearnable" (Fragment 2, 6), "And these have been made own by the power of these things and those" (Fragment 9,2). Τοῖσι … καὶ τοῖς, *words are leading the way toward an image. To an absent image.*

A world of immigrants, of smugglers, of refugees.

If you look at the vase, you will see the many images portrayed by Parmenides' poem on it. Everlasting, and yet absent images. A volute-krater by the underworld painter of Apulia, a vase decorated with all the Parmenidean scenes. At the top, the head of the other goddess. The most ancient goddess. Γαῖα, *the earth-mother. A figure surrounded by creepers, and by thousands of flowers. Then, a lintel, a* ὅρος, *the limit between the visible world and the underworld. Between these two, the many mares carrying an initiated. Leading the mares, young women, Daughters of the Sun. And there are four horses. Always pulling the chariot. If you turn the vase around you will see a naked boy standing in front of a woman. Another woman is putting her right hand on his left shoulder. There is also Justice. And an entrance* (Cf. Trendall, *Red Figure Vases of South Italy and Sicily*, 209).

Right behind the wall that separates Parchappe Avenue from the railway there is an entrance to an abandoned warehouse. What I call an entrance is no other thing than a break in one of the brick walls. The break resembles an ancient gate, an inverted triangle surrounded by piles of bricks, and closed at the top with a steel cornice. That was the entrance to the wine warehouse, to the old technical high school. An entrance to the underworld.

"And the goddess received me kindly" (Fragment 1). She welcomed me without carrying me to the shadows of death, μοῖρα κακή.

The beggars who had slept there overnight have left a trail. The trail leads beyond the triangular gate, toward an arcade or a temple. Carved on its drum columns there are Greek verses talking of the occasional cycles of depreciation that embrace and constrain us all.

He slowly approached the wheel and took a look inside it. He saw his many faces reflected on the water. Then he descended, careless, and waded, with his feet rooted-in-water. A red sun reflecting on the water showed him the many figures of truth, figures whose shape can neither be forgotten nor captured by a camera. There, inside the wheel, "it is the same what you perceive with your eyes and what is in being" (Fragment 3).

Once outside, the destructive light of a splendid sun embraced him and nurtured him. Necessity shackled his body. Justice led his trembling body toward the arcade, where he rested overnight. The arcade they called Delphi.

The whole construction that I named Delphi lies in ruins, almost completely covered by leaves and dust. Only the stepped base of the construction, and the rectangular shape of its contour, remain visible. Two columnar drums lie on the sides of the temple. From there I had a view of the world around: toward the left, the wheel that leads inside the wine warehouse; beyond it, a pool partially filled with rain water and deciduous leaves; and a brick wall that set boundaries with the interior of the factory. As the sun-god did before, I found something quite familiar in these ruins. A place wherein to dwell.

She comes into the room to devour his eyes.

A brick wall without breaks separates Delphi and the yard from inside the factory. It was there that he took the image of a sleeping beggar. That old image captured him lying down on the floor, like a dead animal. A ring of bricks constrained his limbs. A semi-god hiding his face, to never reveal or conceal. An exhausted semi-god. One last image captured the ambiguity of the scene. Like a ploughed field or like a pile of bricks. A sign of ambiguity.

In the vase there are two figures of inquiry, two routes. His body and its decay, a mirror image, the despair of the two-headed men, the second-hand clothes in the pawn houses at Soler street, all of them belong to the path of what is in being.

From the early rays of a sunset, from the immobile ruins that appeared behind the leaves, from the many faces carved on the logs, from the bricks that constrained the limbs of a semi-god's body, there was an imaginary figure that seemed to emerge. His face was covered by the carcass of an animal, the head of Minotaur. I, Minotaur, animal of the siesta. The skull completely hid or covered my face. Only my long hair appeared, and fused itself with the carcass. Yes, yes, Minotaur of the siesta.

"ΠΑΡΜΕΝΕΙΔΗΣ ΠΥΡΗΤΟΣ ΟΥΛΙΑΔΗΣ ΦΥΣΙΚΟΣ" *said an inscription found in Velia. "Parmenides Pyres Ouliades Physikos" I carved on the columns of Delphi.*

Without the images, all the doctrine is unlearnable. And the translation, unintelligible. The goddess is revealing to him what is in being, what belongs to being. A goddess of death and healing. A goddess without name. Θεὰ. *A goddess saying that this forking path leading to conflagration is also the path of being. She allows him to have a look at everything that is in being, at the many things that ... [persist] in being. But she does not strive to persuade him. Everything is available to him, the path of persuasion as well* (Cf. Pausanias, *Description of Greece*, II, 348–355).

His body is thin, very thin. Sometimes Necessity guides it, and shackles it (Fragment 10, 5). But Night receives it kindly.

She shows him the many images drawn on the wall. Nineteen fragments. Six talk about the human body and reproduction, two about strife, one on love, two on the Milky-way, one about the Earth and one about the moon. One addresses death. I never quite render them all.

She walks around the cave and illuminates with a torch the many images carved on the wall. She asks him to look at those images. "Because it is the same what you perceive with your eyes and what is in being" (Fragment 3). She wants him to look carefully. To look upon things which, though far off, are yet firmly present to the mind. A continuum of images, none of which could ever be cut off from being. All these images are one, akin to her. She only feels at home in an underworld full of devaluation (Fragment 5).

The exchange rate and the useless coins. Her laugh, and the despair of traders "wandering two headed ... helplessness in their breasts ... deaf and blind alike" (Fragment 6). All of them spin around when she plays her phonograph.

Soon the figure of the Minotaur turned into the shape of a man wearing a uniform. He received me kindly and persuaded me to follow him behind the mountains. There was only a narrow path through which I edged my way.

There, in the pool, I soaked my hands. My ancient hands like bronze. Being is tactile.

Impassive, she listens to each and every one of his stories. While she smokes, he recites for her. He reads through the fragments, with their secret variations and their allegoric interpretations. He never quite sheds light on their meaning. Instead, he uses his limbs to represent the images. She believes, and she told him once, that his body resembles that of the goddess. A goddess with long, well-shaped legs, but without breasts. He recites the poem once again. A single route, a single story, is still left: that which is in being. Her body, a complete order of decay. Complete or not at all (Fragment 8, 11).

RENDERINGS

Those who claim that being in the pampas is subject to the question of being in general are also compelled to affirm that ontology in the pampas consists primarily in the elucidation and translation of *being* into Argentinean Spanish. Defined in this way, the question of being in the pampas may not differ from the question of being *in any other place* (Cf. Borges, *Other Inquisitions*, 146–148). *Eἶναι* may remain untranslatable in Aristotle's *Metaphysics* as well as *eon* in Parmenides' poem. Being may be thematized in its relation to *the category of place.*

Yet, if we reject this view, we are required to show how being appears in the pampas by means of the ontological notion that place exceeds itself.

Being, it is said, could be rendered as *ser*. But that rendering faces many difficulties, for the primordial meaning of *ser* is *to be seated.* This is somehow odd for a philosophy of motion as well as for temporal ontology, and this may explain part of the disquietude with regard to ontology. Yet, we do not say "being at rest in the pampas," even though we may insist upon the primordial character of stillness.

Indeed, what is the purpose of our inquiry if it is not to ground the political as such? Does it simply remain seated as a mere matter for soaring speculation, one of those questions arising in solitude, about the most general of generalities, or is it rather, of all the questions, both the most basic and the most concrete since it concerns the *placing* of being?

Being in the pampas exhibits the fact that being both takes and exceeds its place. Accordingly, being is *ἄπειρον*, full of motion, untraversable, continuous, familiar, taxable, hyperinflated, depreciated. But doesn't this notion of place run against the idea that a being always occupies its own place, that being is delimited, bounded in accordance with its genus and species, becoming a field for inquiry, a certain definite area and subject matter? Is this the path that temporality has followed in thematizing being?

In acknowledging the fragmentary character of ontology we secure our path toward a land full of hoofprints, stories, gossips, natural catastrophes, mock wars, recollections of generals who died in exile, polysemic grammars, and fictional literature. Yet, not one of these precludes ontology from unfolding itself, or from becoming a theme in Darwin's scientific search for specimens, except by resisting any reduction to temporal categories. The traveler who tries to set boundaries between images, signs, fashion, and mintage falls into that traveler's own trap shortly after, or is eaten by the Indians and *vaqueanos.* Only the political-hygienic, a politics without *πόλις*, has compromised in fixing subject-matters. Science as such, contrary to fashion and mintage, is a late phenomenon in the pampas. There are, however, footprints of science and basic concepts that are seen as proximal clues for disclosing this being in the pampas. Some of these have followed the path of Lafinur's interpretation of Condillac and/or Locke as one and the same person. This wasn't a muddle, or a fancy display of eclecticism, but rather a need to rush ahead and against. His own footprints are not far from those of Darwin, Echeverria, or Hudson: they attempt an account of what is manifest in the pampas, to make a theme of the captive as someone who is always changing into another, becoming otherwise, by collecting rumors and retellings then storing them away in journals and inquiring into the ways in which each particular area has been constituted.

In Borges's essays this tendency is made transparent. Carriego interrogates his life on the outskirts of Buenos Aires, concluding—as Heraclitus did before him—that "the gods are also here."* Being is also displayed on the outskirts of Buenos Aires, and in a unique way: by exceeding itself, by resembling what took place in a German saga. Moreover, this tendency toward writing journals did not cease under economic crisis and a cycle of military governments and depreciation, but actually revealed even further the presence of being in these cycles that compel human beings to live many lives in one—beyond reward, punishment, or faithful truth.

Being in the pampas is manifested in these cycles, in the new coins minted, in the many shapes, in the fact that being did not leave but always circulates and dwells in the pampas. Perhaps we are to understand this idea beforehand, for our analysis will come back to it again, and its repetition will reveal how being is taking place in the pampas. In doing so we are already being carried by the travel journals of many: Calfucurá's notion of politics, Dorrego's being prisoner of his own soldiers, the stern look of the *vaqueanos*. Here the fragments from Eleatic thinkers—Parmenides, Empedocles, and Zeno's works are enough evidence—for they have been read under the premise that what remains to be investigated is the translation from the Greek *εἶναι, ἄπειρον,* and *πόλεμος* by the Spanish nouns *el Ser, lo Ilimitado, la Guerra*. Such an inquiry has been carried out by following a certain notion of historicality that underlies the very foundations of political economy and doxography, a notion that took a different path from that which the Eleatic thinkers follow in dealing with being. On the one hand, the status of these translations comes into question, for their meaning has to do with a certain notion of chronology; on the other, we attempt to shift, to move our attention from temporality to *place*. Our attempt is to depart from the foundations of doxography and to show that the question of being may have always followed an erratic path that is yet to be traced further, but whose outcome has always been displayed as footprints and hoof-prints that leap ahead, that link, that refuse to cut off, that split the very question of being.

Such an inquiry on being in the pampas, then, focuses its attention on the way that time steps out of itself in order to place itself elsewhere, how it shifts attention from temporality and its relation to being to *place.* It posits a radically different kind of inquiry as genuinely ontological. In this shift, what is philosophically primary is the motion, the excess that displays the way concepts have been taken and disseminated. Further, it concerns the history of ontology. It demands that we pay heed to the role of signs and images in such a history of ontology. We attempted this two-fold task before, when we posited Parmenides in the pampas, and we claimed that in reading the fragments that have survived from his poem, we must deal first and foremost with images that unfold to reveal being—images that evoke, recall, and find echoes in the pampas themselves.

If to posit Parmenides in the pampas was a first and necessary step in the task of understanding the way that ontology makes itself manifest there, it did not give answers to the question of the testimonies and collected fragments from the Eleatic school, for the fragments themselves—keeping within the testimonies of many—pointed to the problem of place in any ancient account of being. We are not saying that in their ontological disclosure Eleatic thinkers made manifest their "local colors," or "their local customs." The Eleatic thinkers revealed that being can manifest itself in different places, hither and thither; that the very margins of philosophy are also in being. It would be misleading to take these testimonies as an ontological inquiry that posits only "local colors." Instead, we need to inquire as to the way their premises and their research revealed the notion of excess. What led them to the conclusion that it is necessary to show that what is in being is *ἄπειρον*? In other words: how was it possible to display what is in being and posit the main traces of a path for writing the history of ontology? Being in the pampas, then, is not a linguistic subterfuge, but a root for a whole saga of exiles, murderous actions, mock battles, is rooted in water biographies, anecdotes, gossips that come to fill a void full of excess.

Any development of the question of being in the pampas must use the continuum as the ground for a genealogy of different possible ways of inquiry. Aira has depicted the continuum in terms of this excessive void, linked to the need for retelling, gossiping, launching money, and counting story after story, the story of a story in order to both fill a void and avoid cutting being off from what is present in being (Cf. Aira, *The Hare,* 22). Borges acknowledges this continuum when he says in regard to *Martín Fierro,* that "the dream of one man is part of the memory of all" (Borges, *Dreamtigers,* 40). In this last sense, however, the continuum leaves behind the immediate in order to pursue the universal, for the main problem of many is that of the discontinuity of the territory. But also, in this sense, one can glimpse a certain cruel doubling taking place. Arguably, one learns more about this by looking at people's motions, gestures, and convulsions than by reading the history of ontology. An account of being in the pampas can be traced by following these everyday actions in their external relations (motion, collision, actions, reactions) to any portion of inquiry. These configure the face of the other, its being otherwise, and the chorus with its persistent retellings. Is it in this way that we may come to and display an understanding of what we really mean by the expression "being in the pampas?"

We are entering a land where litigious, frivolous, conceited people may come across gossiping, boasting, rioting, looting, combing their hair, and taking over the notion of being. Still, it is clear that in doing so we are not writing some kind of travel journal that examines the anthropological features of certain "Argentinean characters" or "traits," but are attempting to show the ways being moves through the places of the pampas and exceeds its very being there.

The question of being in the pampas, then, has finally turned into a visible path. A path that may unfold itself as representation from Greek lyrical poetry to Aira's reliance on Huiliche images, and from Galen's account of Parmenides' poem to Macedonio's *siesta.* In establishing this position, the history of ontology will not depend on a certain chronology since any account of being becomes an account of something *already there* or fully present here—a disclosure of things as they have happened and are happening in a certain place, an event that can only be compared to a cruel *mise en scène.*

THE MINOTAUR

Limits, boundaries now constrain her body (Parmenides, Fragment 8).

Borges has left a single image, a semblance of literature in the pampas. An image that holds captive all the sacred texts of the Upanishads, all the Homeric hexameters, and the heroes of the Nordic saga.... They are mirror-images of our bodies. The same may be said about all the philosophies. It is natural to think that Parmenides' poem is one, and perhaps the first of them.

In her body all is full of light and obscure night together. Everything is shared by them (Fragment 9).

They like to take portraits of their families. He has developed many photos for them, but not all. There are in the developing dish some trembling images of a woman that he may keep to himself. The mechanical eye focused less on her delicate breasts than on the bruises on her arms. She? She could devise love first of all gods (Fragment 13). Love without bruises, or cycles without conflagration.

Sometimes, when he stares at her naked body, he wonders how their limbs are united. Like his thoughts, they are one in a way that they are not (Fragment 16).

After a devaluation, a conflagration, one wakes up, dead on one's feet, from a long dream. Drained and full. One knows, for example, these things: that there are bodies, that they somehow decay, that they may be found in the pictures, and that they were born and now they are. A cycle should be followed by a conflagration that will melt the coins. It is not until then that things come to be and come to an end. It is in this very process, in the turmoil, that for each of these men have established a new and distinctive name (Fragment 19).

He is preparing a class that he is not teaching yet. His notes include the translation of Parmenides' fragments. A classic of Latin American fiction. The legacy of Borges.

I taught in a high school on the shore. I ate and slept there as well, but that only happens in days of depreciation.

I have already lived many complete cycles, some of them at the same time or casually, following a whim. In every case, the circle closed around me. The lack of food paralyzed me and made my body shake. After the convulsions ceased I remained still and blind until I ate again.

By closing the curtains, by turning off the lights, by lying still in bed I came to understand how a body, perhaps my own body, could multiply itself, and depreciate itself infinite times.

Little by little every limb rested and dreamed. Faces that I made out came back to me. Faces that appeared as fierce Greek warriors, or as feminine figures wearing grotesque make-up. Figures from which I could not hide myself. Or it was perhaps that I did not want to. One by one they were taking their place. In successive moments I was each of them. Soon, it was all one to me.

Day after day I walk to the school through mud and sand dunes, the only path available. They need a grammar and literature teacher, but I am going to teach my class as I have prepared it. There is no bus going in that direction. I have to walk.

I keep a photo of that day. I moved into the room, a room with yellow walls and no windows, except those in the double door. A light bulb hanging from the ceiling, and a bed right below it. The bed had a bronze bedstead. The bulb cast light over it, turning everything even more yellow. I bought a table lamp and I borrowed a radio to find out when the next conflagration might be. I kept my savings in my pockets, and the radio on day and night. When the depreciation finally precipitated upon us, I rushed into a diner and ordered extravagant dishes. That day I wasn't frugal.

I might have had some secret happiness in those days. Life was simple, almost plain. Like the land. That happiness lasted for some weeks. Very few weeks.

Fragment 4 says "for you shall not cut off what is in being from holding fast to what is in being" (Cf. Parmenides, Fragment 4). *It is a long fragment that survived in Clement's account. The land resembles the fragments.*

On a cold journey in June I walked through the muddy path toward the school. I had an appointment letter in one hand, the silver camera in the other. It took me several hours to reach the shore. I wished someone could give me a ride, but I saw no one on the way to the shore. It was Sunday.

I think it was during that journey that I pondered the meaning of εἶναι in Fragment 3 for the first time. I was thinking that I did not have any photo of myself, except one from my childhood, when my grandmother insisted on seeing a curandera to heal me from pain. I have never quite forgotten her face.

It was during this walk from the hotel to the shore that I imagined Parmenides in the pampas, in the southern plain lands far away from Buenos Aires. Perhaps because Bahía Blanca has been ravaged, reduced to ruins. To abandoned buildings that the wind has covered with sand and men have painted yellow. Parmenides couldn't find a better place to settle down.

I am recollecting all these images, but I do not keep any photo of myself. In those years I was ashamed of my body. I never quite dare to look at my body in any mirror.

I learned how to use the camera a long time ago, but not from my father. This kind of education is a law in the pampas: gratuitous, incomplete, overtaking. One learned from women. Always. And when you asked after their men, they give an unequivocal answer. Behind the mountains.

Traveler's Journals

Traveler's journals frequently aim to report curious, bizarre aspects of a totality established through the interconnection between paths in the pampas. In this endeavor, not only do these journals trace some of the existing tracks through this territory, but they also display the ways in which what is in being appears to the occasional traveler who, while wandering and in motion, gazes upon the activities of the Huiliches. The traveler is compelled by curiosity to take note of the manners that bring forth a certain regress *ad infinitum:* the concern about mintage, the plain dresses, the trifling matters that bother the inhabitants, the inner rebellion, the contortions of the bodies, and the cruelty exercised over them by bureaucracy. Sometimes, in discovering a hidden path, a certain way of comporting or carrying oneself, the traveler faces a traveler's own destiny: repetition. This is shown in Darwin's journal as we preserved it, as well as in the testimony of Hudson, and the question of the hero in Borges's poetry. A questioning that has been carried out according to Hegel's notes about the *Río de la Plata*. These accounts, remarkably the one of the Jesuit ringing the bell every midnight to remind the natives to perform their marital duties, turn out to be a mockery in a reversed way. It is meant to reveal some particular philosophical "character"—the archetype of laziness unfolding itself and by itself, but suddenly by some excess it turns out to be an ontological disclosure. The conclusion that Spirit took a nap (*siesta*) in the pampas (perhaps its very first *siesta*) has unsuspected consequences, in part because it displays the put-on as a certain irony and a certain fearless, insolent use of ontological terms. These journals also attempt to construct a continuum out of incidents, but in such an attempt they neglect the question of continuity itself, except in the case of Hudson, who becomes part of what he describes.

Raising the question of being in the pampas as one of place, journals appear as tablets giving a report on a κοῦρος's perceptive understanding, not only because the journal follows a strict procedure of forgetting and recalling everything as it has been seen, but also because the recollection becomes part of what is recollected such as when the *κοῦρος*, the initiate, is interrogated; when the *κοῦρος* is compelled to answer the many questions while seated in a chair of Memory. This recalling, we need to note, is not out of kindness but out of cruelty—travelers, initiates, members of the chorus, witnesses, hares, captives, bank accounts—all are equally subject to a right of inspection* (Cf. Fernández, *Macedonio: Selected Writings in Translation*, 83; Artaud, *The Theatre and Its Double*, 116–21). This censorship, this excessive interest in knowing what the traveler saw and heard, begins by reading what was written down in a tablet, a sort of journal, but this ontological curiosity turns into additions, rumors, retellings, into turmoils that spread from place to place, and "establishes a continuity between different places and times" (Aira, *The Hare*, 39). Being in the pampas, then, means first and foremost being immersed in that territory and coming to understand the cycles of alteration and depreciation. For a while, the *κοῦρος* becomes a loud-mouthed storyteller, with some special distinctiveness in his tongue, who brings what is also in being into light in a provisional way. Our discussion must turn its attention to this process one more time, for *κοῦρος* has been described in terms of traits and things present-at-hand that do not necessarily exceed themselves: "an old sword, a leather frame containing the daguerreotypes of a blank-faced man with a beard, the dash and grace of certain music, boredom, solitude and inactivity to a remarkable degree, ... a never ostentatious nationalism" (Borges, *Ficciones*, 167).

Again, what makes the *κοῦρος*'s journal distinctive is not only its poor individualism (Borges), its rage against the hyperinflation of the State (Macedonio), or its observations with regard to the individual's right of mintage (Aira), but the fact that the journal becomes and exceeds the image of itself. In its very being in the pampas, a tablet, a journal may display, show, exhibit, and reveal the continuum of being. This is shown in Parmenides's poem in its motion and inner tendency toward the performance of intricate contortions and loud, well-inspired thoughts, which denote the gratuitous excess of being in the pampas, and which prefigures that any newcomer, *recienveni-*

do, initiate, κοῦρος appears in a relation to excess or satiety with regard to this particular being in.

When Pindar linked due speech and moderate eating, drinking, dancing, and love-making by means of πέρας, he was not only trying to caution the Greeks against the excess, the surfeit that may lead to insolence, and ultimately to a revolt, to the upheaval against time itself, but was also pointing it out as an ἐπιφαινόμενον: beings take more and less place than themselves (Cf. Pindar, *Pythian Odes*, I, 82–84). Historical ontology, indeed, interprets this ἐπιφαινόμενον as a concern with regard to the length, the due time, of any recital. Indeed, the excess was—judging by the many testimonies—one of food, of bodily movement, most particularly, of the stomach. What appears in Greek thinking, then, is an inquiry with regard to beings and being *qua* being: the excess, the insolence, the possibility that things may exceed their place. This very notion, which is manifest in Hesiod's *Theogony* (591–593), unfolds a certain closeness between richness, lavishness, surfeit, and opulence of being. Yet this disclosure was overtaken soon after, and thematized within the boundaries of time as an issue regarding the construction of theater plays. Aristotle's *Poetics* provides an answer to the disquietude around long theater plots that may satiate an audience who, in turn, can become insolent and violent. His temporal accounts of the κόρος relate such insolence to the violent contortions of the body displayed in a scene, to a spectacle that may exceed the proper pleasure (Cf. Aristotle, *Poetics*, 1453b14). Theater representation, whose main concern has been to display actions on stage, became subdued to time, to the arrangements of the plot: "The spectacle, while highly effective, is yet quite foreign to the art and has nothing to do with poetry. Indeed the effect of tragedy does not depend on its performance by actors, and, for achieving the spectacular effects the art of the costumier is more authoritative than that of the poet" (Aristotle, *Poetics*, 1450b27–32). Time appears as the main concern with regard to the display of being in Athens: "as regards length, tragedy tends to fall within a single revolution of the sun or slightly exceed that, whereas epic is unlimited in point of time" (Aristotle, *Poetics*, 1449b7–8). What did this shift in time imply for the primordial display of ontology? Is it within this temporal framework that the display of actions is excessive?—"the incident of Hector's pursuit would look ridiculous on stage" (Aristotle, *Poetics*, 1460a15).

Such a view, too, in its general lines is not alien to the ancient Greek poets: *κόρος* is also related to stillness, which does not deny the excess, the very possibility of excess, but prevents the risks of falling into it. This shifting was also displayed in the Pythagorean thinkers and compelled them to arrange being in columns whose gathering together remains hidden (Cf. Aristotle, *Metaphysics*, I, 986a15–986b10), and to work with the one as good only insofar as it is limited (Cf. Aristotle, *Nicomachean Ethics*, V, 1106b29). This tendency is the one that the goddess without name is fighting against. Eleatic philosophy exhibits a tendency toward the reasoning that we know as regress *ad infinitum* when it speculates on the excessive character of being. From there, it is but one step to the continuum between the *κοῦρος*, the traveler, and the captive, for in these there is a certain rapture, a certain "being carried away" always given in advance.

In Parmenides' *poem*, the *κοῦρος* shows a remarkable interest in recalling details of his journey. The whole poem is a detailed account, an effort to summarize within the limits of hexameter the many things that the *κοῦρος* saw and heard, the many things that are present in being. Pausanias observes that the procedure is preceded by a double bath, a bath in the waters of *Λήθη* and a bath in the waters of *Μνεμοσύνη*. The scope of that procedure is to give in advance, to make visible a way of understanding being-in, namely, that of astonishment.

The tragic events of New Rome, indeed, show the kind of violence that this procedure may carry. Olivieri's stubborn decision to postpone mintage—or rather, to refuse to be involved with this practice until other forms of excess were also manifest—and the refusal of the soldiers to put themselves to work led to famine, despair, the murder of Olivieri, and the end of the colony. However, we should not infer from here that the many cycles ceased. To a certain extent, the excess was displayed in terms of traces, retellings, fragments, fashionable clothes, all of which pointed toward the many cycles that one must live in order to repeat a past life. We can find echoes of this distress in Borges's *The Babylon Lottery:* "Pythagoras recalled having been Pyrrho, and before that Euphorbus, and before that some other mortal. In order to recall analogous vicissitudes I do not need to have recourse to death, not even to imposture" (Borges, *Ficciones*, 65). Murderous attempts, convulsions, hunger, and fashionable clothes display the uncertainty involved in the *ἄπειρον* character of being. These paths were not only manifest in Borges, but also in Macedonio's exploratory analysis of stillness and Aira's account of the political problem of the discontinuity of the territory. All of these converge into the image that life constitutes an impossible taking place in the pampas; for life shows itself as something both greater and lesser than itself and as exceeding its own feasibility in ways that it does not: revolts, changes of fortune, journeys, a lover, an affair, rapture, the loss of all our savings, the fact that death itself finds an author who is after it, etc. But life itself has been a theme for stories that presuppose a notion of reductive temporality: an over-emphasized existential mourning that treats the chorus as a mere *they* and bounds place to nothingness.

The question of being in the pampas reveals the political problem of the discontinuity of the territory. The continuum gets extended only by the many links, the arbitrariness of the connections, and the necessary inventiveness to exhibit what is in being. The many cycles of depreciations and the many languages brought by immigrants also contribute to make certain understandings of uncertainty occur. They show that the many cycles of depreciation lead toward the question of cruelty as a mode of doubling, of unfolding in place. Ontology, in contrast to philosophy, faces depreciation as one of its concerns (Cf. Aristotle, *On Coming to be and Passing Away*, I, 314a1–315a25). It claims that "being is hyperinflated," or "being is depreciated." These claims dwell in truth. These claims do not require that the ontological structure of depreciation in the pampas should be theoretically transparent, but at least made explicit in the phenomena to be analyzed: mintage, signs, fashion, and images.

Thus, in claiming that traveler's journals point out that depreciation determines the character of the question of being in the pampas, we are not making claims with regard to the privilege of writing, or of literature as a means of displaying the excess of being. Parmenides' poem should be understood in terms of the images that it evokes, displays, and calls for. In Eleatic thinking, particularly in Zeno's paradoxes, there is a tendency toward the continuum of images, toward a regress *ad infinitum* and an insistence on the fact that these images unfold being as *place;* that in their repetition they themselves—and not time—link, mingle, imitate, or fold back into themselves. Such an ontology of *place* does not reduce the question of being in the pampas to a question of a stock of images standing in reserve, and the collision between them. If that were the case, the continuum could be reduced to a *montage* of representations as suggested by any historical account of being. Eleatic thinkers revealed that beings always exceed their *place,* that they are untransversable, *ἄπειρον.* Their excess is given in advance. Juan Dahlmann, for instance, "chose the line represented by his romantic ancestors, his ancestors of the romantic death" (Borges, *Ficciones,* 167). His death was foretold by his ancestors' death. He finds a continuum—secret or manifest—between them, even though fully aware that he would die in the pampas and not in the marshes of Germany. This continuum raises the problem of ontology as repetition (*Wiederholung*). Did ontology follow certain paths without cutting off what is in being? What was the place of *time* in such a historizing of being?

Traveler's journals not only exhibit ways of being in the pampas. They also show the discontinuity of the territory. The recollection of hexameters, bucolic poetry, and obscene rhymes converges with photography in that all of them use images for cutting out fragments of reality by means of a lens, and by doing so reveal a continuum of what exceeds itself. These images, these recollections trace a certain path, yet they do not set clear boundaries between themselves and the accounts that thematize being in the pampas in terms of *civilization* and *barbarism.* In these last accounts, what takes place is an historical shift, for what matters is not *place* but the way time—most likely, the future, the later—has traced a dialectic between two opposites that is to be overcome. Further, both Sarmiento and Martínez Estrada needed a philosophy of "characters" (the gaucho, the *vaqueano,* the *rastreador*) to thematize being in the pampas without making explicit how these frequently exceeded themselves, becoming otherwise than themselves in their dwelling in the pampas.*

Indeed, their accounts made visible that being in the pampas is a problem of *place.* But if this is the case, it may be asked, why might our notion of *place* as *ἄπειρον* be different from Sarmiento's or Martínez Estrada's accounts? Isn't it also a problem of montage? In inquiring about montage we should note that in a chronological account, *time* itself is what deals with montage. On the other hand, in an account based on *place* images themselves organize the montage by mingling, extending, exceeding themselves, carving the bodies, twisting, imitating, resembling, etc. Images themselves constitute the continuum. A continuum whose frame remains untraversable.

In situating Parmenides in the pampas we attempted to make manifest a sort of continuity between beings. We let the images and the fragments move freely—displacing, moving, turning over themselves. This motion was understood to display a certain overabundance, a surfeit of entities in being. In this we glimpsed the possibility that being always crosses boundaries, that being is unlimited, and that the things that are in being are also excessive, they have "too much being for such and such space." When we presented Parmenides, we did so in devaluation, but that turned out to be a celebration of the fact that everything is in being, for we wanted to show that what is called the underworld, the world of devaluation, is also a phenomenon that takes place and compels beings to engage in their cruelty. As Cafulcurá puts it, "it's simply a matter of seeing everything that is visible, without exception. And then if, as obvious, everything is connected to everything else, how could the homogeneous and the heterogeneous not also be linked?" (Aira, *The Hare*, 26). Ontology, then, like any economic theory, must seize upon the notion of *ἄπειρον*, of excess.

Indeed, at first glance it seemed an anachronism to place Parmenides in the pampas, for how can a thinker who lived twenty centuries ago come to live in a rancho? There is also a difficulty in taking for granted our rendering of the *poem*. We did not specify any particular step toward an understanding of Parmenides' fragments, except by saying that there are paths, and some paths are the way of non-being. Our rendering of *εἶναι* as "what is in being" or "what is fully present in being" makes manifest that in her truthful speech the goddess intended to display images as excessive, as "having too much being" (Cf. Fernández, *Selected Writings*, 20). Besides, the understanding of Parmenides' poem is delusive, as the very question of its meaning runs ahead, so long as we do not think of Parmenides' poem in term of fragments.

Indeed, temporal ontology conceives the fragments as cut off from reality by means of a lens. They occupy a certain *place* in the *poem*. Their own place. The whole question of the interpretation of Parmenides' *poem*, then, should be preceded by the arrangement of the fragments. The question of being becomes, then, primarily a question concerning the link, the connection of the fragments with regard to a conjectural arrangement of the many pieces. Further, and traditionally, ontology affirms that Parmenides' fragments have to be organized as a discourse, as a double speech. We learn: this is the way of Truth, that is the way of Seeming, preceded by a poem whose content should be *allegorical*, not in the sense of pointing at something else that exceeds the poem, but in that its true meaning underlies what is displayed by the images, which must be put aside, or thematized as poetic artifices that are used to give a certain importance to the speech itself. The poem then becomes merely successive, conjectural, allegorical.

Doxography has managed to preserve the fragments, to detach them from certain secondary sources that kept them—Simplicius, Galen, Aetius, or Plato—regardless of the fact that those thinkers were following a certain path in thematizing them. For they give an account of the fragments in terms of *place*, of the excess that the whole poem carried from here to there, from Velia to everywhere else. Manifestly, Aetius placed being within his concernful understanding of medicine, Galen within the realm of astrology as a question that took place in Athens. Plato himself needed to posit Parmenides in Athens before asking the very question of the meaning of the Eleatic doctrine of Being. The fragments themselves exceeded their *place* and dwelled in many other places, moving hither and thither. In other towns, in other voices. In the many rumors, in the retellings and misunderstandings of many people.

The history of philosophy insists on the goddess being a poetical fiction, and takes for granted that the whole Eleatic journey toward being is a device made up to hide a theory of logic with two terms: being and non-being. Scholars amuse themselves with scandalous delight at the impossible: a goddess who claims that she may talk about truth, but her words turn out be on other topics, such as war, reproduction, astronomy, naming practices, rituals, fashion, and economics. Temporal philosophy refuses to acknowledge that the fragments point to images, that when the goddess says ... τοῖσι ... καὶ τοῖς, "to these things and to those" she is pointing at, displaying images of "what is in being" (Cf. Parmenides, Fragment 9). It is only by taking into account the question of *place* that we can give a serious account of the cave as a place for learning, something that has been repeatedly described by Greek travelers like Pausanias.

The problem of being in the pampas exceeds that of the *reception* of Eleatic philosophy. It is a problem of understanding how these fragments take place in the pampas, and how they exceed their being there. Thus, the problem of reception is not merely a problem of the translation of *εἶναι*, but concerns the excess of place that being is taking where the translation is to be made, for some images may be already there, evoking, echoing, displaying being-in. Thus, the decision to posit Parmenides in the pampas, and to trace the doctrine of the Eleatic school in thematizing the question of being in the pampas are not arbitrary. It is not a nationalist account grounded on the mere fact that Parmenides was a native of South Italy. The political as such behind the very question of *being* is the question of the untraversable excess of being, its being *ἄπειρον*.

When Borges posed the German saga, when Macedonio claimed that Hobbes visited him in Buenos Aires, and when Aira advanced the problem of meaning in the Huiliche tongue as ontological, all of them were acknowledging that being is taking place in the pampas both as something accessible to us and as something to be understood and interpreted. The question of being in the pampas becomes an inquiry on translation as long as translation itself takes and exceeds its place. Primordially, the question of being in the pampas is the question about how the notion of being unfolded itself as the notion of the continuum, a notion that in itself "prevented the Huiliches from giving clear and precise definitions" (Aira, *The Hare*, 27) and is one that addresses the problem of how to follow these paths and hoofprints through the many cycles of changes, depreciations, and defaults that have been taking place in the pampas. For, besides the fragments, the discontinuity of the territory, and the incongruence that ties up the images in the continuum, there is the question of the One. We ask: how is it possible that all these are One?

Calfucurá's answer offers a perceptive understanding of the problems involved: "It's simply a matter of seeing everything that is visible, without exception" (*The Hare*, 26). Or again, it is a matter of acknowledging the excess of being displayed by images, for in giving ourselves the task of solving the paradoxes we are to deal with the problem of enframing in the pampas. It is not only a concern about technology—enframing—but about the other of technology, the cow, mintage, bureaucracy. Are we, then, going to follow a path, "not just an ordinary path—the path that certain animals take when they leap in a zigzag fashion, if you follow me; although at the same time we ignore their detours to the right and left, which due to a secondary effect of the trajectory end up of course not being detours at all, but a particular kind of straight line" (*The Hare*, 27)?

When Heidegger asks after the frame and finds that the essence of technology itself is enframing (*Ge-stell*), he attempts to move away from a notion of time as conceived by technology, or with regard to the essence of technology.* In doing so he faces the question of the frame as something that exceeds itself, that cannot, and must not be seen as a boundary for the question of being. The Huiliches also ontically think of framing as a montage of series of fragments. But in their view, the continuum is montage itself. The fragments themselves configure a continuum by the fact that they exceed themselves. We should not infer from this that the continuum is the essence of technology. In the continuum it remains a question about the collision, about the zigzag fashion, about cruelty and representation. In spite of this, or rather for this reason, we are to display, to exhibit the continuum. Thus, when asking the question about being in the pampas, or what is to be in the pampas, we are not merely asking how to render *εἶναι*, for *εἶναι* asks for images and is always pointing toward them. Images are always ontologically closer to us. Yet *εἶναι* has been ontologically farthest in any temporal account of being in which time, as being, steps out of itself. Thus, in asking the question of being in the pampas we are not only to deal with an etymological analysis of *εἶναι*, or how *εἶναι* became *ser*, or how *ser* became the emptiest of Spanish verbs. We claim that to answer the question of being in the pampas implies finding the images, the signs, the coins, and the clothes that display the continuum, even if this path may have a zigzag fashion.

This thematizing of being can be found in Macedonio's inquiry, "what is it that I have before me, then? Phenomenon, being in its full reality, that is, color, sound, texture, temperature—phenomenon, occurring in being, that is to say, neither inside me nor outside me" (Fernández, *Macedonio: Selected Writings in Translation*, 19). It is not only that Macedonio seems to recollect, to write down on a tablet what he saw, what he heard in the presence of being: he is also asking us to open our eyes to variety as the continuum that exceeds itself in multifarious forms, in the way that the open-eyed variety overwhelms the waking consciousness by being "everlasting /

individual and memorious / without beginning, without break, without end" (*Selected Writings*, 20).

Being in the pampas, then, turns out to be a question concerning representations, enactments, and performances on a catwalk: the pampas. In this exhibition, images would abolish the distinction between scene and auditorium by acting as forces reflecting back ontologically upon their own cruelty.

The history of ontology, then, can be represented by a chorus, and its inner tendency toward *κόρος*—toward excess and satiety—is already manifest, carrying itself and anything else, moving the scene, defending the territory, claiming, carving, doubling, shouting, looting, minting ... *εἱλίποδ' ἀκριτόχειρα*, "with rolling gaits and countless hands" (Empedocles, Fragment 60), disclosing the fact that decay, depreciation, change have always taken place in the pampas, even before the default. Thus, "like reality" also means "being," which in turn means "free," "without law" (*Selected Writings*, 22). Ontology, then, is to be conceived in terms of "repetitions, clarifications, reversals, mutual contradictions, rejections" (*Selected Writings*, 25) of any report on "everything that is," what in turn reveals that being in the pampas is "plenitude of being," that which exceeds the mere "appearance or representation of something else" (*Selected Writings*, 25). This is what Macedonio has thematized as *awareness:* "perceptual awareness, being, is one, continuous, selfless, and substantial and utterly knowable" (*Selected Writings*, 26).

We have to secure our access toward the excess of being by tracing the notion of excess in Eleatic thinking in such a way that it will make clear that its contribution to Western thought has been the idea that being cannot be cut off from being, and that beings should be looked upon as exceeding their being.

Our first step, perhaps, is to free ourselves from any skeptical account of Eleatic thinking as a philosophy of immobility. Eleatic thinking relies heavily on images, and on reasoning by regress. We have to note that Eleatic thinkers took care to avoid the question of *time*, for chronology could cut off what is in being from holding fast to what is in being. They took care to display, to show that being gives *ἄπειρον* signs: countless signs, untraversable signs.

Further, we have to show that Eleatic philosophy's main concern was that of *place*, that being both takes and exceeds its own place. It may be objected that this interpretation of Eleatic thinking runs against the accepted view regarding what these thinkers said, and that such an attempt is also grounded in a certain politics with regard to the territory. Admittedly, in following such an interpretation there is a risk of falling into a certain irrationalism, or confused interpretation of being. Furthermore, any attempt to give an account of Eleatic philosophy needs to deal with the fragmentary nature of the sources: it must offer a different interpretation of the way that the fragments have been arranged.

In detaching ourselves from historical ontology we depart from a conception of time as that which subordinates events to their *own place*, and that which separates alteration from coming to be and passing away. Chronology not only relies on conjectures concerning the dates offered by multiple accounts of the life of Eleatic thinkers, but also on a certain understanding of the way some commentators preserved the Eleatic texts. It is sometimes suggested, for instance, that Aetius's *Placita* is an early attempt to give a strictly chronological account of the life of philosophers. But in doing this we forget that Aetius's text was also concerned with the question of place. His *successions* are an expression of the thoughts conveyed somewhere else (South Italy, Ionia), and that is the reason why the philosophers are linked by a continuum of rather whimsical, bizarre, bewildered images, hesitations, rumors, and retellings. What is there to say, then, of Hyppolitus's scandalous claim that Empedocles, Heraclitus, Plato, and Aristotle were Pythagoreans?

Reducing these accounts to chronology forgets that in linking these philosophers, thinkers were engaged in trying to trace a continuum, addressing the excess of what had been thought there and here. What seems to be shallow, spurious, frivolous, irrelevant to us was in fact the primordial concern for those thinkers: the continuum between ontological disclosures according to where these took place.

With Aristotle and his disciple Theophrastus, the question of *time* gained attention as a primordial way of criticizing the compelling tenets of earlier thinkers. Aristotle himself, however, also went to great lengths to show that Zeno's view of being was the ill-grounded product of a misunderstanding in regard to place. Aristotle understood quite well that for Zeno being is excessive and that for Eleatic philosophy being always exceeds its own place, but the *Physics* is an attempt to ensure that every object exists in its own time and takes its own place. This understanding explains Aristotle's attempts to cut off being from holding fast to what is in being. Indeed, we must remember that Aristotle does not see Zeno as a skeptic but as a dialectical thinker.

The notion of *place* leads us to inquire as to the *in* in the pampas, for this *in* displays a two-fold character. Conceived as *ἄπειρον*, being *οὔτε σκιδάμενον πάντηι πάντως κατὰ κόσμον / οὔτε σινιστάμενον*, "neither disperses itself in every way in order, nor gathers itself together" (Parmenides, Fragment 4). The notion of *place* is an ancient one. Its becoming ontological in Eleatic thinking is yet to be thematized. With the onset of a *temporal* distinction, which classified beings as *temporal* entities (natural processes and historical happenings) and *non-temporal* entities (spatial and numerical relationships), the notion of *place* that underlies the Eleatic account of being is eclipsed, fully subordinated to the notion of *time* as before and after. In Aristotle, for example, we find an insistence on confronting Eleatic thinking with the idea that things must happen in divisible time. By means of *time* Aristotle ensures that beings are to take a bounded place. This move can only be paralleled, or rather completed, by his claim that truth itself—Eleatic philosophy disclosed by means of images—is to be found *in* assertions, between their temporal and non-temporal belongings. Truth itself, then, appears bounded (*accorralada,* rounded up) by assertions.

It is also our plan to show how Aristotle's notion of *place* leaves room for a temporalizing interpretation of the Eleatic thinkers that is still visible among us, but which was rejected or at least objected to by the so-called Hellenistic or *eclectic* philosophers. Their "eclecticism" has to be understood as an attempt to posit again the notion of *place* since they were aware of the problem of cutting being apart from itself. We have yet to display these traces but for now it is necessary to understand that this other conception of philosophy held sway for more than seven centuries, and its last exponents were not Simplicius or Philoponus. These many philosophers were engaged in a serious and systematic attempt to challenge the *placeless* meaning of being, as well as the *ὅρος* character of assertions. How did it happen that the very notion of *place* as posited by the Eleatic thinkers turned out to be simply being *in this place* or even *in space*?

Place, in the sense of *being somewhere,* functions as a criterion for distinguishing realms of being, and when inquiring about the meaning of being in the pampas we realize that being's path has become a sine curve (Cf. Aira, *The Hare*, 189–206) where the problem displayed is that of the discontinuity of the territory. How did this phenomenon come to be in the pampas? Is its ontology rooted in excess or in the speech of the goddess? Can we claim that *place* has its roots in some sort of feminine conception of ontology?

From the standpoint of temporality, things show themselves in their temporal character as long as they exhibit themselves as entities *in a place*. And still, *temporal* cannot simply mean "being in this or that place," for time also exceeds and lacks itself. What is to be sought is an interpretation of the *in* that makes manifest the excess of being, for it is in that *in* that the frame of the question of the continuum lies.

It is frequently said that in modern metaphysics—especially with Descartes—this notion of *place* is often subordinated to *time*. Kant, for instance, who was aware of the problem of *place*, reinscribed it within the notion of *sublime*. The sublime comports itself as an excessive, overwhelming, inexhaustible "being-there," as *Dasein* (i.e., as lightning observed from a certain distance, there), that in its excess moves our dispositions—twisting us, turning us backward—and in its excess compels us to always be more than *Gemüt*. Thus, the sublime in itself echoes a note of exceeding itself by being "equal only to itself" (Kant, *Critique of Judgment*, 105).

Further, the modern use of the term *place* is closely related to "space of representation." Even if we do not necessarily subscribe to this meaning, we may need to show how this notion of "space of representation" takes place in the pampas. In other words, why did the *in* not carry in itself any idea of theater, of cruelty, when speaking of the pampas? Why has *place* been understood as "objects in a certain place" and yet "not exceeding that place?" Didn't this notion already present a binary polarity between *civilization* and *barbarism*, assigning Buenos Aires to the former, and the pampas to the latter?

It is necessary to exhibit a link, a continuum between the notion of *in* and that of *ἄπειρον*, in such a way that the Huiliches' reasoning *ad infinitum* is fully explicated as relying on a continuum given in advance that continuously exceeds itself: "the hare runs, but by definition it must run across territory. If for example it is running on the continent, it cannot be running on the island. But then, if it takes off and lands on the other side of the channel separating the continent from the island, then it is doing so, isn't it?" (Aira, *The Hare*, 34).

At Harding Green

He does not have an image of his body, of his entire body, yet.

In the poem, the maidens covered their heads with veils before entering into the house of Night. This image bothered me for a long time, perhaps because I came too late to Bahía Blanca, after the (failed) foundation of Nueva Roma, when men lived in caves for years. So many years that their relatives in Buenos Aires forgot about them and, believing them dead, split their inheritance.

It was when walking to school that I conceived this translation, "For it is the same what you perceive with your eyes and what is in being" (Fragment 3). It was not painless, for a couple of crabs bit me on my feet.

Yes, it was in the path crossing the crab shallows. My feet sank deep into the mud. No one saw me, except a woman. A woman who witnessed how the crab shallows can be crossed without a vehicle. She didn't recognize a familiar face on me, not at all. She did not know about Parmenides, or about the bites on my feet. She never asked.

It was inside the building used as a school where I found the woman staring from behind the window at anyone who crossed the path. She received me kindly. She almost offered me a cup of tea.

I also took one look at her. I looked through her at a glance. She introduced herself as the principal, but I understood at that very moment that she was not a woman of titles. So much smoking had turned her voice hoarse. What I heard was a rough sound, a bottomless echo. She smiled, compulsively arranging her combed black hair, carrying in her look that indifference of those who know the ropes. Behind her back appears the image of the Libertador. He didn't bother to look at me.

After I taught my first class I included material that was not in the syllabus. Students didn't ask for the poem until weeks later.

The room was brightened by the soft radiance of a dim bulb. The radiance cast many shadows on the wall. I paid attention to them in rendering the poem, for Pausanias said that the initiated learned by looking at images and by listening to an ancient god. It was easy for me to understand what he meant by looking at images in a dark room. Above, a wood ceiling covered everything with dark night. The walls were salty and dry, like any other wall in Bahía. The images were not.

Women teach everything. Everything, except how to take photos. I learned it by myself, by reading books, Daughters of the Sun.

Currency depreciation takes our savings. We must accept this fact. Completely, or not at all. I need to tell you how it happened. It was not my idea. One day she asked about the meaning of τάδε *and* τοῦ δε*, and after pondering long enough she said that there must be some images to which the words are pointing. That these couldn't be mere words.*

That—justice, perhaps—is rooted-in-water. One always bathes on the shores of Λήθη*, in the muddy waters of the Río de la Plata.*

But also, the pampas is the perfect place to get away. One is suddenly no one, or everyone. No one will ever inquire about one's past. Instead, they will add profuse details to it. That is their right. There, I am Parmenides, the poem, the Libertador, the mud.

Argentine Spanish is a language for traveling. That is why people grasp a language like English so easily. There is no substantial difference between them. Depreciated coins, whose exchange value has been lost. We take for granted that something changes. The idea that language is complete, ungenerated, is a scandal produced by a pretentious thesis. They fiercely repeat the verbs and their conjugation: amar, temer, partir. *Yet, no one uses these ancient forms. These verbs are archetypes. They have the manifest attribute of summarizing an entire life. Naturally, there is always a problem of order, of priority. One needs to find out, by looking back into one's own life, which precedes the others. That is the difference in destiny, the roots of our poor individualism* (Cf. Borges, *Other Inquisitions*, 33–35).

They begged for photos. Their silver bodies also, their many sexes, κοῦραι.

In the shipwreck they lost their dignity and composure as much as the color of their eyes. Soon they took local women in marriage, I heard. They had children with the color of the land (copper skin, squinting eyes, or vice versa). They also adopted that foreign habit of drinking heavily. As many others did before. As the gauchos did, and before them the workers of the railroad, and the conquistadores, *and the Indians. Unlike the rest, sometimes they committed suicide. They said that it was because of the harshness of the winter, the dust carried by the southern wind, or the unbearable lack of trees. They drank just to forget that they had already forgotten and had been forgotten. They fear the extension, the flatness of the land.*

Some have dug a tunnel from Zelarrayán street to the Cathedral. They said that it is because they fear the Indian raids. And then they repeated on and on, more or less from memory, the story of the captive boy, an Indian boy with blue eyes (Cf. Echeverría, *La Cautiva*; Aira, *The Hare*, 24–45). *They lived for months, for years in that passage. Eventually, they lost any recollection of the sun.... They created their own cosmogony grounded on the lack of light. They learned how to write on the walls, and how to read by using their hands.*

It is because of them that this writing has so many contradictions. For they were my avid readers, and the cruelest censors.

The History of Ontology

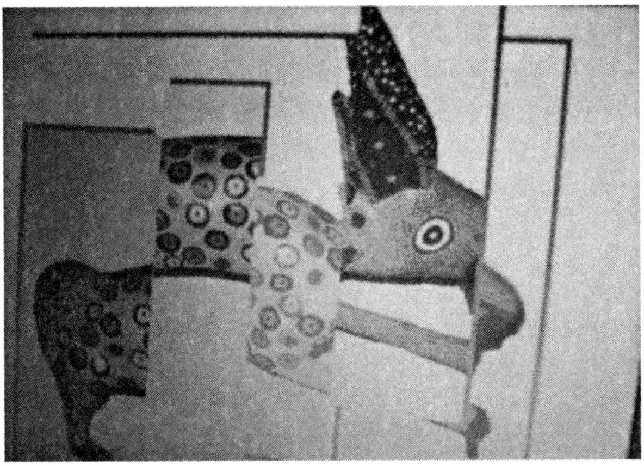

History, it is said, is the frame within which being is depicted. But the Huiliches' notion of the continuum is also a frame; not in the sense that it allows a succession of stories to be established, but in the sense of observing that the *images themselves*—the many signs—establish a continuum by exceeding their own places. While a temporal account of the story of the captive, for example, implies giving an account of transformation—changes in the color of the captive's eyes, nationality, and sex—nothing is more natural to conceive of than the fact that these changes take place and that they exceed their proper place for the delight, the celebration, the laughter of the Huiliches. The political problem of the Huiliches, that of the discontinuity of the territory—whose epiphany is the alteration of currency—is to give an account of those extraordinary transformations in such a way that these can be seen as one. Mintage and censorship have transferred their excess into that account.

Further, we may affirm that place lays the ground in which time itself is conceived; the discontinuity of the territory is linked to the many cycles of economic depreciation in such a way that our bodies are doubled, multiplied, cruelly compelled to exceed themselves. Yet, the condition of that historicizing is uncertainty, and its product is frequently a recollection full of excess that is utterly manifested in cycles: "Like all men in Babylon I have been a proconsul; like all, a slave; I have also known omnipotence, opprobrium, jail" (Borges, *Ficciones,* 65). One is compelled to acknowledge these past lives. Their recollection is eventually surmounted, surpassed by an invitation, or rather, an imperative that is already implicit in the notion of continuum. Any author, any one engaged in retelling such historicizing "authorizes any further writer whose temperament and circumstances favor intense labor to correct and edit it freely, with or without mentioning my name. The task will not be small. Delete, amend, change, but, if possible, let something remain" (Fernández, *Macedonio: Selected Writings in Translation,* 95).

In asking the question of being in the pampas we attempt to unfold the roots of a tradition that runs from Eleatic thinking to Huiliche narratives, and from Plato's allegory of the cave to the events of New Rome. In doing so, we have to wander back into fragments, through the many clues transmuted in the retellings, and whose curiosity makes itself manifest in the excesses of different and divergent accounts showing being in its multiplicity. It is only by providing a theory of the way things are conveyed from one place to another that ontology can acknowledge the changes, the depreciations, and the default as present in being (this is the path from place to being). The history of ontology, then, becomes an *ἄπειρον* account of that excess, of that surplus that relies on gossip, on echoes, turmoils, and rivalry.

Our program, then, is hyperinflationary in nature, and in a way that it is not, for in tracing back the notion of *place,* in asking the question of being as the question of being in the pampas, we are always to include more and more voices, retellings to the point of making manifest that even after *ser* became detached from place and state, it can only be conceived as a void full of excess, inexhaustible. Maps, journals, testimonies denote such a tendency. The notions of circular time, freedom of mintage, and fashion already make implicit the assumption of the hyperinflation of being. But the question of depreciation, alteration, itself has been hidden, forsaken, or forgotten by a chronology of things over and done with.

Images have also been forgotten and, under the same regime, acquire an equivocal status as abiding mental representations of a "subject" or as synthesizing a manifold of experiences. If the allegorical is real—as Rosas conjectured—images are not only carved in this or that place, or painted on this or that wall, but to be found everywhere and anywhere, even outside of his daily dreams. Images proliferate, uncontrollably, always in motion, always asking for another fragment. In reaching such an understanding we need to acknowledge within the history of ontology Simplicius's discussion of Aristotle's *Physics,* with regard to the latter's response to Eleatic conceptions of place. His way of dealing with the Eleatic texts was one of deleting, amending, and changing what was written, and indeed, also allowing something to remain.

The question of being in the pampas seems to be placed within a familiar land, and yet the path we are following is an unfamiliar one. In addressing the question of being, Argentinean writers have often followed the path of idealist philosophy, and idealism puts the question of *time* ahead of the question of *place*. Indeed, idealism prioritizes images as a means of gaining answers to the question of being, but links this question of temporalized inquiry with regard to the status of representations, images, or ideas to the "connection" between these and the sensory experiences, leaving aside incongruence (that of dreams, and that of alteration).

Hudson, perhaps following the path of Berkeley, recollects his dreamlike trip to the pampas: he never thinks of motion in terms of temporal links but as a traveler's journal full of episodes that could happen in any other order. The connection between events is always related to the fact that sensory perceptions are linked by means of excess, what temporality considers to be mere interruption in the sequence of before and after. As for alteration, the colorful bills that Espina issues are backed up to the absolute. He presupposes the excess of their value, he is aware that once in circulation those bills will exceed their nominal value, that they will follow a flow of depreciation. Likewise, in Tlön, the value of the nine copper coins is in question not because of the succession of representations itself, but because of their depreciation *in* time. The Tlönists argue so to deny "the misleading detail 'somewhat rusted by Wednesday's rain'" for it may entail admitting the continuity, the very reality of these hyperinflated coins (Cf. Borges, *Ficciones*, 26–27).

When we are talking about the montage of images, we do not need to presuppose a connection, a temporal link between these images in such a way that motion is *understood* in terms of *before and after* and enframing becomes a riddle, a technological problem of essences, in which excess is suppressed and a clear cut collection of images is presupposed as resulting from the succession. From this point of view, the task we are facing seems formidable. We are to show that Parmenides' fragments rely on images and sounds, but in doing so we should have already proved that it is the excess of the image itself that creates continuity between them. In positing the question of being in the pampas, then, we have to focus our attention on the *in*, on the very notes that made this *in* excessive, dense, hyperinflationary. Besides, we need to deal with an issue with no delay: we need to provide some account of the circulation, alteration, shift of the meaning of being in the pampas, in such a way that makes it possible to display the traces of the foundation of circulation itself: mintage.

The *in* as thematized by the Eleatic thinkers can be traced in the pampas insofar as we display the detours, the turmoil, the cruelty surrounding the fragments, for in these the *in* steps out of itself. In the continuum we are in the midst of an ontology with numerous filiations and distortions that determine the conceptual character of ontology even today. Eleatic philosophy is its own fragments, reduced to a clarification of the notion of the One. It is a recent event that ancient philosophy became a fixed body of doctrine; an event in which every interpretation, every attempt to move forward from the traditional reading of Eleatic philosophy was left aside or fixed by forbidding any attempt to delete, amend, change something within its fragments.

Present-day philosophy rejects this view rather dogmatically, as if "the Greeks" were unconditionally "Greeks," a "race," or "the people." We focus on their chat, whose ontological disclosures neither disperse themselves in every way nor everywhere in order not to gather themselves together in their retellings. Early thinkers have shown awareness of the continuum of events that happened here and there. It is problematic, then, to think of Greek ontology in terms of doxography—a conceptualization that detaches our concerns from those of the Eleatic thinkers—in terms of a certain chronology that makes us forget, that hides under a veil of testimonies the fact that the fragments are also thematized in the testimonies. This ontological view is also displaced in the way that we still think of philosophy in terms of *time* but elude the question of *place* as the primordial way that ontology thematized being, or as the way that thinking spreads itself and exceeds its boundaries. The efforts to unfold these notions also followed the same direction, for in asking the question of being, in phenomenologically thematizing *Dasein,* instead of doing so in terms of a *there* that exceeds its place and circulates, it became a *Dasein* whose concernful understanding is grounded in time.

Perhaps our first task in clarifying the question concerning being in the pampas is to examine how the interpretation of being turned away from *place* at a certain point in the history of ontology, and took shape as a question concerning the *temporality* of being, a concernful engagement of philosophy with the question of *time.* In doing so, we are not going to trace back the unfolding of temporality in present-day philosophy, but instead, we will suggest some of the turning points, certain twists and turns of the paths that detour from the temporal frame. We can find these paths in ancient ontology and in modern philosophy as well. Manifestly, this is the case in Kant's notion of the *sublime* as an excessive, "partially analyzable" concept, evoking a certain failure to comprehend the "absolutely great."* To understand the notion of the sublime in Kant we need to trace back the question of *place* as *Dasein,* as a notion that runs against, challenges, and opens up temporality into the idea of *space for representation.* In doing so, Kant glimpses the presence of a chorus, always moving, unfolding, contorting, rolling on the floor, creating its own *space of representation.* A chorus that suddenly makes manifest in ontology itself a continuum, a chorus that gives us "everything that is in crime, love, war, madness, if it wants to recover its necessity" (Artaud, *The Theater and Its Double,* 85).

It is in Artaud's writing that we find numerous signs, clues of the notion of the continuum. His writings on the theater of cruelty show that being as taking *place* always "gives room" and takes more and less place than itself, opening a "space for representation." Indeed, his claims—particularly, the claim that "everything that acts is a cruelty"—have not been well understood. When he talks about an idea of theater that has been lost, he is really displaying, advancing the main traces of a history of ontology as "the agitation of tremendous masses, convulsed and hurled against each other," a history of ontology grounded on "famous personages, atrocious crimes, superhuman devotions" (*The Theater and Its Double,* 85). In many interpretations, Artaud's disclosure steps back into a mere notion of the theatrical. In raising the question of being there are at least three things we must do: in the first place, with regard to the translation of being we have to inquire how being itself "spreads its visual and sonorous outbursts over the entire mass of spectators" (*The Theater and Its Double,* 86). Second, we have to posit the question of the sources, the voices, the fragments that compose that ontology, and to show how ontology itself, that is, the astonishment of being, becomes a theme.

The first thing Artaud says about the themes to be represented in the theater of cruelty has to do with *κόρος,* for "it is not a matter of boring the public to death" (Artaud, *The Theater and Its Double,* 93). This precept may evoke that of Pindar's poem: the audience may reach a certain point where it gets distracted, and being full of satiety, they may become insolent and violent; but in Artaud's view, the chorus is already full. Satiety is given in advance as a primordial forestructure. The chorus is full of *κόρος,* and it must furnish "the spectator with the truthful precipitates of dreams, in which his taste for crime, his erotic obsessions, his savagery, his chimeras, his utopian sense of life and matter, even his cannibalism pour out, on a level not counterfeit and illusory, but interior" (Artaud, *The Theater and Its Double,* 92). In Aristotle, on the other hand, we lack a thematizing of the chorus. In a laconic paragraph, he mentions the fact that such a loud-mouthed gang entered into the polis late, when the theater was already installed, and when the political took necessary measures to prevent the surfeit. "Indeed, it is only quite late in its history that the archon granted a chorus for a comic poet" (Aristotle, *Poetics,* 1449a3–b4). What is so dangerous about the chorus? Its assertions? Its "truthful precipitation of dreams?" The fact that the chorus may raise any ordinary object "to the dignity of sign?" (Artaud, *The Theater and Its Double,* 94) Why are actions to be first and foremost temporal actions? What is the status of the chorus with regard to the history of ontology?

The chorus spreads being by giving to "words approximately the importance they have in dreams" (Artaud, *The Theater and Its Double,* 94). Artaud seems to install words beyond the temporalizing analysis made by Aristotle; beyond that which is in time and that which is beyond time. Artaud's views contrast with the temporal arranging of the plot because he is proposing an excess in which the catharsis is given in advance, already taking place. This ontological insight detaches Artaud from the question of how long a play should last. Later we will ask whether his resistance to temporality is not to be found in Terence's comedy, or in the *Trauerspiel.*

Λήθη

Before I came here I knew how to forget. The procedure is simple, so simple.... Pausanias writes that one only needs to immerse oneself in the muddy water of Λήθη.

Humans are not supposed to spend so much time in water. One forgets almost everything. Yet one learns how to laugh right after, and how to let them write one's recollections in hexameter.

Greek etymology might vanish away our uncertainty. But then, it would be difficult to lie (Cf. Aira, *The Hare,* 120–151). *That is why they think of truth as an agreeable fiction.*

I already had the camera when I thought that the poem must be accompanied by images. That there must be a torch illuminating the many figures on the walls covered with lime. Yes, I had the idea and I tried to reproduce these images by taking photos.

You may wonder why Parmenides came to this land. It's hard for me to think otherwise. And I am not alone on this. Borges has a story about devaluated gods, a thesis advanced by Hudson more than a century ago (Cf. Hudson, *Tales of the Pampas;* Borges, *Other Inquisitions,* 141–145). The Purple Land *is a later tale, undoubtedly, but this fact does not deprive it of its merits. For Hudson wrote it when he really became extended, part of the land, when he could not flee from the underworld. Suddenly it was natural for me to think that he was part of the pampas. Nowhere else can one be cruel and unpunished. No matter how many children one might eat, there is always someone who ate more. And so on* ad infinitum.

ARISTOTLE

In the *Physics* Aristotle raises the question, in what sense is it asserted that all things are One. His response seems to be grounded in contempt toward the Eleatic thinkers—particularly Parmenides and Zeno—for their display of excessive reasoning, and because *these* are "impossible, yet they are far from being identical" (Aristotle, *Physics*, 185a25). He focuses his attention on the ontological claim that "Being is infinite [*ἄπειρον*]" as the ground for claiming that place exceeds itself, that place—and beings—are *ἄπειρον*. We may notice that while for Plato, Eleatic philosophy is to be understood as a philosophy according to which "being is greater than itself and less than itself," for Aristotle this lack of limits, of clear boundaries, becomes an obstacle along the path toward the very inquiry on being *qua* being.

Aristotle replies to Parmenides' claim that being is a continuum by suggesting that if we are to think the continuum, we should see that their One (the Eleatic one, the One from that place, Elea) "is many, for every continuum is divisible without limit" (*Physics*, I, 185b10–15).

We may notice that in his interpretation of the Eleatic thinkers, Aristotle bounds their opinions within the limits of assertions, *ὅρος*, and that he disregards the way that Eleatic thinkers had thematized images as ways of unconcealing, of revealing the *ἄπειρον* character of being. Once he makes this dual move, Aristotle can then discuss *place* as a category of being. It has been noted, indeed, that the discussion of *place* in Aristotle is preceded by a discussion of the question of the *ἄπειρον*, which Aristotle relates to the temporality of being. Instead of an exhibition of how being takes place Aristotle offers an inquiry: "what is place?" His attempt at defining *place* then ensures that beings cannot exceed their place, that beings are not *ἄπειρον*. Thus, *place* is what contains or is contained.

In his temporalization of Greek thinkers, Aristotle quotes Hesiod, whom he perceives as having "accepted the general opinion that everything must be somewhere and must have a place" (*Physics*, IV, 208b30–35). This temporalization of the question of being leads Aristotle to confront the Eleatic school of thought—that group of thinkers who claimed that being is at motion and at rest, that being is greater than itself and less than itself and the other, and that being is *ἄπειρον*—being is that which one can not get through, being is limitless; a school that grounds its reasoning in regress *ad infinitum*. Zeno's paradoxes, which denote this excess of being and a tendency to over-extend place itself, is under Aristotle's gaze. What kind of explanation does Zeno's difficulty demand? Doesn't place need a place? What is the status of *and so on* with regard to being? (Cf, *Physics*, IV, 209a25). To be present in being must mean to be circumscribed to a certain limit. In what sense, then, is something *in* another? Aristotle's circumscription of being offers several options not grounded in Greek grammar, but in the idea of a temporal limit of being. Being, it is said, is: (1) *in* the pampas as a hare is *in* it, as parts are in the whole; (2) as the whole is *in* the parts, like when one is in debt; (3) as a gaucho or the captive is *in* mankind; (4) as the captive is *in* the tenterhooks; (5) as Pellegrini's face is not minted *in* this or that bill; (6) as a child is *in* her mother's womb. As (7) the existence of a thing centers *in* its good and generally *in* its end, i.e., "in that for the sake of which" it exists; and finally and in the strictest sense of all, (8) as a thing is *in* a vessel, or savings are *in* a bank (Cf. *Physics*, IV, 210a15–25).

It is clear from this list that being is in itself, and it never exceeds itself, that being is neither more nor less than itself. Thus, Aristotle can flee from the regress *ad infinitum:* "We shall now have no difficulty in escaping Zeno's dilemma that either there is no such thing as a place, or it must itself occupy a place; for there is no reason why the proper place of a thing should not be 'in' something else—only not in the same local sense as that in which its content is 'in' it" (Aristotle, *Physics*, IV, 210b22–30). From then on, being is thematized within temporality. *Place* is not *ἄπειρον* any more, but (1) becomes what contains that of which it is the place, (2) place is not part of the thing, (3) the *immediate place of a thing is neither less nor greater than the thing,*

(4) place can be left behind by the thing and is separable. Temporality also ensures a proper place for beings, a place within *ὅρος*, (5) all place admits of the distinction of up and down, and each of the bodies is naturally carried to its appropriate place and rests there, and this makes the place either up or down (Cf. *Physics*, IV, 211a1–15).

The first four claims that Aristotle makes in his temporal analysis of *place* run against the primordial disclosure of the Eleatic school. Being, the being of beings, is not excessive, no longer *ἄπειρον*. Beings have boundaries, limits, and neither a being nor its place exceeds itself. But this way of conceiving ontology contrasts with the Eleatic "you shall not cut off what is in being from holding fast to what is in being," and with the disclosure that being "neither disperses itself in every way everywhere in order, nor gathers itself together" (Parmenides, Fragment 4).

An objection can be raised at this point with regard to being in the pampas, for any disclosure of the ways being unfolds itself in the place of the pampas depends on a certain understanding of *place* given in advance that runs against Aristotle's third claim: *place does not extend beyond itself*. This difficulty is even clearer when we think that in an historical ontology we are to deal with the question of the reception of ontology in the pampas, with the rumors, retellings, the very way by which philosophy spreads itself through the territory and exceeds the pampas. If being does not extend itself, the question of being comes to be a question of "locality" and community. We are in danger of falling back into the interest of the community in its own literature and its own national philosophy. We may even risk falling back into an anthropological account by historicizing being itself into a philosophy of "national character" and "Argentinean traits" (Cf. Borges, *Other Inquisitions*, 33–5).

The very possibility of the continuum is something to be elucidated. Meanwhile, our task is at great risk. If being never exceeds itself, if *place* itself is always "neither less than nor greater than itself" it is difficult to explain how being could ever be disclosed and unfold itself in the pampas. We may say, for instance, that the continuum seems to take place due to some kind of *motion*, for the Huiliches move in the territory, and so does the traveler. The hare runs across the territory. According to the logic of the continuum, "if for example it is running on the continent, it cannot be running on the island. But then if it takes off and lands on the other side of the channel separating the continent from the island, then it is doing so, isn't it?" (Aira, *The Hare,* 20). Aristotle himself observes that our speculations on place depend on motion, on change of place as given in advance (Cf. *Physics,* 211a8–15), but he demands that in any inquiry with regard to motion the place of a thing should be equal to the thing itself (211a25). Place, then, is defined as a boundary, the boundary of the containing body must be thought as in contact with the contained body (Cf. Aristotle, *Physics,* 212a5). With this definition of *place* and *in,* the question of being in the pampas is rounded up within the question of "locality."

The question itself may turn around and become "the places of the pampas are in being." For don't we have enough evidence to claim that being exceeds itself in the pampas? What are the consequences of saying, as Aristotle does, that "place is the innermost motionless boundary of what contains" [*Physics,* 212a25–30], that place does not exceed itself and does not move with beings, but rather contains the bodies as a limit which is bounded by time? Isn't this a political decision with regard to the territory, rather than an ontological one? This is, perhaps, the final outcome of chronological ontology. How could being have ever taken place *in* the pampas since *in* cannot be thematized with regard to time?

THE TEMPORALITY OF BEING

If we want to display this thematizing of being in a way that makes explicit that time exceeds itself, we have to turn our attention to Plato's *Parmenides,* for this book offers us a comprehensive view of Parmenides' and Zeno's doctrines that goes beyond the limits of chronology. We may notice, for instance, that Plato's interpretation of the Eleatic One is carried out in Athens and not in Velia. In Athens, Parmenides and Zeno are foreigners who have been received kindly, but who nevertheless remain outside the walls of the *πόλις* (Plato, *Parmenides,* 127C). Why did Plato posit Parmenides and Zeno in Athens as a place for thematizing the question of the One?

At this point we may be tempted to temporalize the question of being by seeking precision in historical events and asking questions such as, did this meeting take place? If so, when? And how? Plato seems to know nothing of this way of temporalizing the history of ontology and surprises us with an almost complete lack of chronology—for how would Parmenides and Zeno travel to Athens at Socrates' time? Was Socrates really present that day? Is Plato making up a story? Is he trying to trick us? Is this a story written in jest? Doxography has turned the subject of being into a serious matter. There is no place for mockery, for frivolity, for digressions of any kind within it, unlike Plato's account which relies on rumors, gossipings, retellings, and voices from here and there.

Plato's *Parmenides* is a story narrated by Cephalus of Clazomenae, about whom we know almost nothing. He recollects the story as it has been told by Antiphon, who in turn did not witness the visit of Parmenides to Athens, but tells the story as he heard it from a direct witness, Pythodorus. There are many voices already installed in this ontological disclosure, many voices always amending, adding, deleting, rejecting, and refusing to talk. And still, we might find ourselves insisting on asking the question of being in temporal terms. Is it by chance that temporality prefers to see that introductory dialogue as a "dramatic setting" without representing it on stage? Do we grasp that Plato is thematizing the question of being with regard to the *in*?

Parmenides opens up the possibility of thinking of the One as that which exceeds itself. It is only in terms of excess that we can exhibit the meaning of his thoughts. Excess, the *ἄπειρον* character of beings, for instance, is given in advance: "If anything comes into anything, it must be not yet in it, while it is still coming in, not still entirely outside of it, if it is already coming in, must it not?" (*Parmenides,* 138d). Being is never completely in itself, but always going beyond its limits: "it cannot be either in itself or in anything else" (*Parmenides,* 139b). But then, the One is neither in motion nor at rest, but elsewhere beyond these two.

Ontology is troubled by this chain of reasonings about being because it assumes that being *qua* being, the being of beings, must take a definite place. How can we truthfully assert that "the one, as it appears, being never affected in a way other than itself or other, is never affected in a way other than itself or other, is never unlike either itself or other" (*Parmenides,* 140b)? or that "the one will be neither like nor unlike either other or itself" (*Parmenides,* 140b)? What is the status of the negations in a reasoning such as, the One "will partake neither of one measure, nor of many, nor of few; nor will it partake at all of the same, not will it ever, apparently, be equal to itself or to anything else, nor will it be greater or less than itself or another?" (*Parmenides,* 140d).

Parmenides is portrayed as teaching the Athenians a notion of being as foreign, untransversable, excessive. It is within this surfeit of being that "the One, inasmuch as it is a whole, is in another; and inasmuch as it is all its part, it is in itself; and thus one must be both in itself and in another.... This being its nature, must not the one be both in motion and rest?" (*Parmenides,* 145e). As he walks along many paths Parmenides' "fresh starts" reminds us of the advice given by the Goddess without name: "you shall not cut off what is in being from holding fast to what is in being," and it is with this advice in mind that we should understand that "the existent One is ... both one and many, a whole and parts, limited and of infinite (*ἄπειρον*) number" (*Parmenides,* 145a). In its excess, being is always "in [a] state of being other" (*Parmenides,* 148a). Given the excessiveness of being we can now understand how being goes beyond Velia, toward Athens, and even beyond Velia toward the pampas.

In Eleatic philosophy, time is excessive; within it being is "older than itself, and younger than itself" (*Parmenides*,152a), and therefore always moving in opposite directions, always becoming the opposite of itself (Cf. *Parmenides*, 155a). So far, we have thematized this motion as a continuum between what has been thought there and what we are thinking here. This continuum is not only a political compromise intended to solve the manifest discontinuity of the territory, but has a more essential meaning. It follows the ancient precept of the Goddess, *οὐ γὰρ ἀποτμήξει τὸ ἐὸν τοῦ ἐόντος ἔχεσθαι* (Fragment, 4). This thought is displayed again and again, from Empedocles' Fragment 11 to the many versions of the captive that we hear in the pampas. "It is like that sad story," says Alvarito of the Indian,

> who was leading his three-year-old son by the hand in some celebration where there were crowds of people. At one point his attention wandered and he let go of the boy for an instant: when he looked again, he had vanished. The only thing left on the ground close to the despairing father's feet was the paper windmill the little boy had been carrying. A kidnapping? Fate? He never saw him again (Aira, *The Hare*, 34).

Can we really say that something vanishes from being? That it is not taking place any more? How could a captive child disappear from what is in being if rumors still wonder about his windmill? In their cyclic nature, rumors spread its continuum: "they seem to repeat or combine events of remote regions, of remote ages" (*Labyrinths*, 73). It goes on, and "it will ever be there wherever or whenever? one may keep pushing it" (Empedocles, Fragment 11).

Being in the pampas offers itself as a question of the *in*. In our elucidation of this *in* we found—through the difficulties addressed by Aristotle—that *in* has a vast range of meanings that are always to be exceeded. For the Eleatic thinkers, *in* means also beyond itself, beyond its boundaries. This is displayed in Plato's interpretation of Parmenides' doctrine, but is it also revealed in the Spanish language? It seems that the Spanish *en* that has circulated for centuries took primordial forms—"*en* reposo," "*en* movimiento," "*en*deudado" concerning both motion and rest.

In the pampas, motion is conceived as motion along a path, a zigzag path traced by many "detours to the right and left, which due to a secondary effect of the trajectory end up of course not being detours at all, but a particular kind of straight line" (*The Hare*, 20). But, isn't this path familiar? Wasn't following this path what compelled Zeno to follow the question of being? Wasn't this Parmenides' journey also? Couldn't this be what we know as the continuum?

The main political problem of the pampas—that of the discontinuity of the territory—compelled the Huiliches to articulate a continuum made up of stories. Stories express an incongruous continuum, grounded on what has been said there and what is said here. The question of *in* becomes one about the discontinuities made manifest by the many paradoxes whose answer must always be found elsewhere. The paradoxes point out that beings are excessive—while in motion and at rest—and that they *have a tendency to occupy more than their own space.* Plato writes, "this being its nature, must not the one be both in motion and at rest?" (*Parmenides*, 145e); the conclusion that is now making itself manifest to us is that "then the one, being always in itself and in other, must always be in motion and at rest" (*Parmenides*, 146a).

Indeed, Zeno's fragments have been preserved within Aristotle's historical ontology. Aristotle himself, in thematizing the question of motion, also creates a continuum between what has been said in Velia and what is thought in Athens, even as the question of being moves away from *place* and installs itself as an inquiry about the temporality of being. *In* is, then, thematized within a temporal framework, circumscribed by *nows*, or instants, that bound beings to their proper place rather than in a continuum in which "any time span—a century, a year, a single night, perhaps the ungraspable present contains the entirety of history" (Borges, *Selected Non-Fictions*, 266).

We have observed that later thinkers did not follow Aristotle's conception of being. Their historicizing of ontology was carried by an interest not driven by chronology itself. Instead, their way of thematizing the question of being focused its attention on the many voices—in the retellings, the heres and theres, the gossipings, and apocryphal biographies. As the Stoics once said to Aristotle in reproach, if the parts of time, of any distance, of a body are not inexhaustible, how are we to establish the continuum in the motion of any object? (Plutarch, *On Common Conceptions* 1078–1080E, in A. A. Long and D. N. Sedley, *The Hellenistic Philosophers*, Cambridge University Press, 1987, V. 1, p. 298).

Scholars, bothered by this thematizing of being, have put these inquiries aside, dismissing them as marginal accounts that have nothing to do with the business of philosophy. As a philosophy that hasn't gone to school "for a long time." They have turned the question of being into a question of the chronology of being. Even the more primordial questions are asked in terms of a *Dasein* who is temporal. Any philosophy that attempts to detach itself from temporalizing ontology has to be engaged in the task of thinking the nature of these sources in terms of *place*, in terms of what is taking place here and there, for "to dominate on the stage the objective expression of gestures and of everything which affects the mind by sensuous and spatial means is to turn one's back on the physical necessities of the stage and to rebel against its possibilities" (Artaud, *The Theater and Its Double*, 71).

When Simplicius objected to Aristotle's definition of *ὑποκείμενον πρῶτον* he was doing so in the name of this other thematizing of being that conceives of being as excessive. Simplicius conceived the prime matter as an indefinite extension, instead of definite length, breath, and depth; he focused his attention on Aristotle's hesitation, "but when we take away length and breath and depth we can see nothing remaining, unless it be the something bounded by them" (Aristotle, *Metaphysics*, VII, 1029a17–22). But Simplicius's definition is not yet understood, and it will not be unless we make an effort in advance and understand that beings take more and less place than themselves, that they always exceed themselves. The diffuse and indefinite character of this prime matter is not to be thought as something ontologically negative, but in terms of *ἄπειρον*, and it is in this sense that Simplicius conceives it as very close to non-being.* Further, Simplicius makes explicit the tendency to conceive *place* as matter, for both of them display *ἄπειρον* as extension: both are indefinitely (*ἀόριστος*) diffuse, and slackening (*πάρεσις*). Place, then, is not to be thought of as one of the categories of being, but as the very "first subject." (Simplicius, *Commentary on Physics*, 537, 19–22). Thus, in ontology we should start by asking the question of *in*, the question of *where*, taking the *in* as a guide that leads toward a continuum in the discontinuity of the territory. Being displays itself in the pampas as long as *in* means "that which exceeds itself in itself" as Plato suggests, "that which is not in motion nor at rest," and "*ἄπειρον*." Thus, the question of being in the pampas turns out to be an exhibition of cruelty, of insolent doubling, of extravagant and lavish continuity between what has happened there and what is happening here. The history of ontology, then, is defined by a proliferation of retellings, opinions, distortions, additions, and footnotes that carry the question of being beyond itself, as "projections and precipitation of conflicts, as turmoil of philosophically distorted and impure manners" (Artaud, *The Theater and Its Double,* 51). This explains our claims that being is depreciated, hyperinflated, and yet continuous, excessive, fully present.

Within this conception of being as excessive, a conception that can be traced back to Borges's and Macedonio Fernandez's works, time exceeds itself in its cyclic nature, but this turns out to be an imperative upon us: to exceed and go beyond ourselves. Yet this imperative is not to be thought in terms of the "Argentinean character," but rather against it, or beyond it. Instead of asking the question of the *possibility* of being in the pampas, we are to exhibit the many ways it already is, the many ways it displays itself; in doing so, we do not adopt a mere phenomenological method by means of which we grasp what is given to understanding in advance but show that what is given in advance always exceeds and takes more place than itself.

The Eleatic philosophers advanced this idea of the unfolding of being in their discussion of Pythagorean principles. This discussion has come to us through Aristotle, but it may remain hidden because Aristotle's account—as has been noticed many times and for different reasons—is already marked by a shift in the understanding of motion, time, and place. Moreover, the fragments of Eleatic philosophy survived for centuries in the later account of so-called Hellenistic philosophy. It is curious that we are not interrogating the derogatory name that covers up six or seven centuries in the history of ontology. Still today, when scholars refer to Hellenistic philosophy they think of those philosophers as mere followers without creativity, and full of eclectic taste, seeing nothing more than absurdity in their excesses. But their bewildered interpretations, their made-up biographies, their inner incongruencies, their retellings, are ontology. These are the unfolding of being *qua* being, and it is precisely because of this excess that Eleatic thinking can take place in the pampas. We must make explicit that its survival was granted by many voices, in many sometimes contradictory and whimsical accounts. Why did every account of the preSocratic thinkers invariably start by mentioning their place of birth? Why all this turmoil about their biographies? Hesitations, retellings, amendments, mistakes, fake biographies have been the rule in any account of philosophical thought. What is there, fully present, "between their lines" in Diogenes Laertius's retelling? "It was Amenias and not Xenophanes who led him to the peaceful life of a student [*εiς ήσυχία πρεάπη*]" (*Life of Eminent Philosophers*, IX, 21–22). Isn't there a betrayal and more taking place in saying "he became the pupil of Anaxagoras and Pythagoras emulating the latter in dignity of life?" (*Life of Eminent Philosophers*, VIII, 56). Isn't this the logic of the continuum? What other link but the continuum of being is there for this incongruency? We need to postulate that these fragments always exceed themselves by themselves. But, in doing so, aren't we incurring the fallacy of finding in our own findings what we have posited in the very beginning of our search? Aren't we leaving room for a regress *ad infinitum*? And still, we have to continue moving along this path to show how being is taking place in the pampas.

Expressions such as *continuum, hyperinflation of being,* and *excess* are methodological, not because they characterize the *what* of the objects of philosophical research and define it as the subject-matter, but because they display the *how* and the *in* of that research. When we claim that *ἄπειρον, incongruency, κόρος* are suitable terms for research on being in the pampas, when we claim that the way that being has displayed itself in the pampas has in turn led to the political issue of the continuity of the territory, we are addressing the history of ontology as unfolded by writers who were "constantly creating continuities, and so adept were they at this that they no longer even needed to employ visible or virtual connections, but simply used the continuity itself to perform that function" (Aira, *The Hare*, 33). It is self-fulfilling to ask why that is the case, and we are to content ourselves in displaying how there is this continuum.

ZENO

In Eleatic philosophy the question of being becomes a question of *place*, an excessive expression: being exceeds its own *place*, steps out of itself and spreads itself into other places, takes place. Being is limitless, untransversable, *ἄπειρον*.

In the process of creating this zig-zag path into Western philosophy, Zeno wrote a controversial treatise on the One. A treatise that defends the notion of One as excessive, *ἄπειρον*, and beyond the boundaries of motion and rest. This is revealed not only in his terms but also in his use of the regress *ad infinitum* as a method of reasoning about being. Ancient thinkers understood his arguments accordingly, and they never assigned to Zeno skeptical thoughts, such as denying motion, or pointing out the unreality of time.

In his own interpretation, Plato needed to pose Zeno and Parmenides in Athens, as a way of expressing that being itself would take place in Athens. Contemporary interpretations forsake all these introductory retellings as gossip and rumors instead of thinking of them as settings for cruelty. Such interpretations focus their attention on the evidence we do or do not have for claiming that Zeno visited Athens by demanding that these passages should make evident the year when Zeno "flourished": he visited Athens when Socrates was "very young" (Plato, *Parmenides,* 127c), which somehow matches with the date established by Diogenes Laertius; with his being Parmenides' "bosom friend," "the inventor of dialectics," and "tall in stature" (Cf. Diogenes Laertius, *Life of Eminent Philosophers,* IX, 25–30). For doxography, the question of being in Athens is whether such a meeting took place.

Indeed, doxography takes pains in trying to set all the rumors aside. Zeno came from Velia. He is said to be a Pythagorean. According to Strabo, he was engaged in political activities. These are retellings, pure gossip out of curiosity. Did he intend to write a book defending Parmenides against those who made fun of his One "by showing that contradiction follows from these other arguments?" How could such an interpretation take place if not by following Aristotle's interpretation of Zeno's argument—that of the divisibility of time? Scholars, then, feel compelled to answer that Zeno was defending some sort of Parmenidean monism.

Such an interpretation takes away the images and forgets that in Eleatic philosophy being is always fully present, always fully displayed in lavish images that spread and unfold themselves. Why do we insist on depicting Zeno as denying, instead of asserting; deceiving, instead of opening up; defending, instead of postulating? Any reduction of Zeno's ontology to a sheerly temporal account will result in a failure to understand the achievement of his philosophy. Zeno (and Zeno's journey through the pampas) will be missed as long as we close our eyes to a certain excess as a note of Eleatic philosophy.

The question concerning "Eleatic monism," as posited by doxography, is unsettled by the fact that Zeno did not use *reductio ad absurdum* to "attack pluralism" (Plato, *Parmenides,* 128d). Instead, he relies on infinite regress in his arguments, showing that a plurality must be both like and unlike in such a way that they become One. If this is the excess presupposed by Zeno, then the conclusion that should follow is that things *exceed* their multiplicity, their being plural, what is granted in advance by Parmenides' notion of ἀποτμήγω (Cf. Parmenides, Fragment 4; Plato, *Phaedrus,* 261d).

Zeno expressed himself in statements that reflect the ἄπειρον, the unlimited, inexhaustible character of being. His One can only be conceived as exceeding the One; any other conception would bound being to be nothing more than itself. He is not skeptical, he does not claim that plurality is impossible, but that even plurality exceeds itself, exceeds its own multiplicity, and that is the reason why he thematized the notion of limit (πέρας). Contrary to contemporary interpretations grounded on a temporalizing notion of ontology, we need to show that for Zeno beings exceed their own being, they are both one and many, both small and large, so small as to have no size, and so large as to be unlimited (ἄπειρον).

What Zeno wanted to make explicit is that any regress *ad infinitum* presents the essence of being; even if *simpliciter,* the argument displays the continuum as exceeding itself. This argument is also manifested in the notion of *ἄπειρον*, a notion that, even though Zeno uses it in one of his arguments, remains neglected for the most part by ontology. *Απειρον* can be rendered as "infinite" but our interpretation suggests "that which exceeds itself," "boundless," "unlimited," "that one that goes beyond its limits" as better renderings of its meaning; and it is in this sense that the paradoxes of the pampas have derived from the Dichotomy, the Achilles, and the Flying Arrow. To take seriously these paradoxes, then, is to acknowledge the excess, the surplus, the hyperinflation of being, and to resist interpreting them skeptically. Once we leave the infinite in the dust of our footprints, we can make explicit, we can display that *ἄπειρον* appeared as *inexhaustible, vast, boundless, without limit as far as the eye can see.* Those are the attributes of being. Why did Aristotle detach himself from this Eleatic being? Was it a political decision with regard to the enclosure of *ἀλήθεια* within *ὅρος*? Why should it "follow" that there is no motion from saying that "it will always have to cover the half, and then the half of the half, and then the half of that, and so on without limit without limit before it gets there" (*Physics*, VI, 239b10–15)? Should we say, rather, that motion must exceed a simple crossing "half the distance" to go even beyond what is *ἄπειρον*? What are the consequences that unfold from the claim that "you can never get there, because you would have to pass through in infinite number of points" but to admit that in order to get through that distance you have to be at the finish line already? (Cf. Aristotle, *Physics*, VIII, 263a5) What Aristotle unfolds in the concession that time itself is infinite is that time does not take place all at once, that time is not ek-static.

The *Achilles* is no other than a demand for excess to take place all at once: that is the only way to understand that "the slowest as it runs will never be caught by the fastest" as untrue. What, then, prevents us from seeing what the paradox displays but a logic of temporality within which any reasoning relying on excess is fallacious? Are we sure that Aristotle is not granting the excess to Zeno when he argues with regard to time that "time, as much as space, is divisible without limit and with respect to this capacity is illimitable" (*Physics*, VIII, 263a10–15)? Why is ontology so skeptical about reaching the finish line?

The conclusion is that to reach the finish line one must exceed oneself and one's place in such a way as to overcome the intervals, and at the same time, exceed oneself in many intervals. Thus, it is not the case that one cannot complete a motion, but in doing so one is already beginning one, and exceeding oneself, giving gestures, images, beyond themselves. That is the way that Zeno postulated motion. He does not attack the view that there is motion, but the way that motion had been thematized, for such a notion of motion assumes that beings, that being itself, should be bound, tied up, settled. To resist Zeno's conclusion, one has to show that motion is not excess and that motion can be satisfactorily thematized in terms of temporality by of categorizing motion within place. This has been the failure inherent in Antisthenes the Cynic's interpretation of Zeno's paradox, for Eleatic philosophy is also grounded in that which is in being, on the goddess's claim that what one sees with one's eyes is also what is in being. But, isn't this evidence used to posit the political problem of the discontinuity of the territory?

The Huiliches's paradox of the hare makes explicit the difficulty involved in any reasoning that denies *ἄπειρον* as an ontological attribute. Reymacurá's reasoning already involves the notion of excess, that place must take more place than itself: (a) the hare runs across a territory, (b) the territory is discontinuous, (c) if the hare runs on the continent, it cannot be running on the island, (d) "but then if it takes off and lands on the other side of the channel separating the continent from the island" the hare runs also over the island, (e) but then ... (Cf. Aira, *The Hare*, 33–34).

In this reasoning, isn't (c) what traditional ontology presupposes? Isn't the discontinuity of the territory overcome by and within the Huiliches' paradox? Some scholars have noticed that perhaps Zeno intended to say something else, that "we cannot get through either of these sequences by going through its members one by one" (Long, *Early Greek Philosophy*, 146). But they find this reasoning too disturbing or too threatening to be pursued. The ontology presupposed in their reasonings prevents them from taking seriously that things take more place than themselves, that for Eleatic philosophy beings are excessive, and that for Zeno it is possible to find another way to take them and get through all, and that is what he called *ἄπειρον*.

Even when scholars acknowledge that this is the case, that any being "presumably ... occupies a space larger than itself," they turn their attention to the divisibility of *time* in terms of before and after rather than to *place* for thematizing this notion of excess. It is said, "if we construe time t as an instant, then Zeno is claiming that things in motion stretch.... But it is not clear why Zeno should think that motion necessarily involved stretching" (Long, 148). Why do we cast doubts on this conclusion? Isn't it also fully manifest in Plato's conclusion that Being must be both greater than and lesser than itself?

Scholars, however, thematize Zeno's paradoxes following some of the patterns of Aristotle's criticism; and consequently they think of motion in terms of *nows* and before and after. One may notice, indeed, that Zeno does not refer to time in his paradoxes, but instead to motion and place. Why is his solution so persistently unheard? What is the politics behind this ontological decision? How does this political move take place? How does this gesture unfold itself into the pampas? What is depreciated?

Cruelty as Imperative

How, we might begin to wonder, did the association between the idea of being in the pampas and the pampas as a space of representation arise? Was it related to the fact that *ser* became an empty verb? Thinking about being in the pampas may lead us to focus on two phenomena always disclosed in advance—the continuum of stories and the cycles of fashionable depreciation—even if, at first glance, these two appear to follow separate paths. Even if the first seems to link events that took place in a historicizing of ontology grounded on *place,* and the second one addresses the alteration, depreciation, and display of the lavishness of being. Following this dual path, the question of being in the pampas recovers the notion of *place* as it was posited by Eleatic philosophy, in terms of the *in.*

When asking what is the meaning of being in the pampas? we are making explicit what present-day philosophy has made implicit. By adding "in the pampas" we obstinately posit the question of *place,* and in doing so we begin to follow a specifically chosen path instead of an arbitrary one. We ask, how does being exhibit itself in the pampas? in the very same way that Parmenides asked, how does being exhibit itself in Velia? Because we hear the concern of Strabo and Diogenes Laertius with regard to giving an account of the place from which Parmenides came once, we liken Parmenides' poem to a traveler's journal—a travel journal that reports his encounter with the goddess without a name, the goddess who says "what you see with your eyes is also in being." What these thinkers found striking in Parmenides' poem was the excessive character of being. But how should one thematize continuums such as the one established in Fragment 8 when it is already fully explicit in the imperative "for you shall not cut off what-is from holding fast to what-is?"

When thinking about the thinghood of beings, we must not separate this one from that one. "This" and "that" are displayed and display themselves as images painted on the walls of the cave. These images are images of being, of what is *in* being. As long as we remember this imperative and this display, we begin to take our steps into the question of being in Eleatic philosophy and in the pampas. In both cases we are dealing with a display, a performance, an exhibition of what is in being with regard to the continuum. But we will not really be on our path until we talk of being in the pampas in terms of cruelty, in terms of doubling and exceeding what is already given there in that territory. The notion of being is linked to the notion of the continuum. The goddess who is addressing Parmenides gives this continuum in advance: What is in being is "all together, one, continuous" (Fragment 8), and again, being "is all continuous; for what-is is in contact with what-is" (8, 25). The account of the goddess imposes an imperative upon us, specifies a way of comporting ourselves toward being, where "it is not right for what-is to be incomplete."

Ancient thinkers acknowledged that the "essence" of philosophy is this continuum. Their historicizing includes retellings, the many voices gossiping about what is in being here or there out of curiosity. In their works we can trace a dual tendency. The first toward the inclusiveness of *whatever you see with your eyes is in being itself.* Everything you see, everything that takes place, is *in* the continuum of being. The second toward interpreting Parmenides' poem as exceeding the poem itself. At that point, what we may call referentiality must also go beyond itself, for the goddess is pointing at images. What images? Images of being, images of what is in being. There is a succession of images that follow, or rather give in advance, the many topics that were just unfolded. But the goddess thematized them in a continuum that includes truth: reproduction, fashion, astronomy, death, love, and naming.

Diogenes Laertius, Simplicius, and Strabo preserved the Eleatic fragments as displaying cruelty, as demanding for us to exceed our being, as giving us "everything that is in crime, love, war, or madness" (*The Theatre and Its Double,* 85). Ontology then must display being as fully present, "around famous personages, atrocious crimes, superhuman devotions, a drama which, without resorting to the defunct images of the old Myths, shows that it can extract the forces which struggle within them" (*The Theatre and Its Double,* 85).

The controversial fragment 3—which for Heidegger contains a notion of philosophy unfolded, lost, and in need of being recovered—is a passage illuminating the difficulty of temporally thinking the *in* in terms of excess. When we look at the history of ontology we are not proposing its *Destruktion,* and we are not just seeking the primordial thoughts of Eleatic thinkers as thoughts to be recovered in order to understand the notion of being in the pampas. Our historiological scope goes beyond this point, for we are suggesting that in thinking the history of ontology we must consider the way that being took place here and there; how being exceeds its place in Velia, and how being takes place *in* the pampas. But, what does this *in* mean with regard to the history of ontology? Once we displace the *in* from chronology, once we conceive of being as otherwise than in time, we have to deal with a sense of a hazy indefiniteness that surrounds the many voices, echoes, and images of being. Can this *in* be displayed in the pampas? Can we exhibit, at least tentatively, the cruelty involved in this excessive *in*?

Clytemnestra

The entire path was covered by water. Suárez tried to push the truck out of the mud but he lacked strength. Suddenly, it abandoned him. Perhaps, there was too much water around. He asked his wife for help, he asked Momo. He was not heard. His feet felt cold, his hands almost frozen. And, from that moment on, he couldn't see beyond himself. Night embraced it all. Dark between tears and a windy voice. Stuck. Stuck in the mud. As his own life was already stuck into his many roles. An actor, yes.

A heavy rain shed his tears. He went back into the truck. He didn't say a word. It seemed to him that life has to be heavy, unbearably heavy to be real. Nothing light can step out of itself. But nothing can be left behind either. The land asked him to get rid of his clothes, plots, dreams if he wanted to continue his trip. It asked him to be light. He could leave Momo as well—for Momo never talks and never helps.

Momo was, in his eyes, the chorus. A mute voice asking, always begging for a role. But Momo had found his place a long time ago.

Suddenly, Martha looked at him, deep into his eyes. He was completely into his own thought and yet waiting for a lightning flash to light the land. To see the pampas. The continuum.

And she may have pondered upon it.

During the following morning the *paisanos* spread the rumor of an unparalleled wonder, that a statue of the mother here and another in Dorrego there were struck by lightning on the same night. Fearful, they pondered this sign and they decided to slaughter all their cows.

They were carried on horseback by the gauchos, leaving behind the truck in the mud. Her clothes, his plots, Momo's dreams, all discarded, left behind. The *paisanos* left them in the only hotel in town, and as soon as they dropped them off, the paisanos disappeared back into the pampas.

The women of the town received them, not without suspicion. He addressed them politely. First he told them that they were a theater company. He introduced himself, then Martha, then Momo. Since this produced no visible reaction from his hostesses, he said that he came from behind the mountains. Not until then did they offer them something to eat.

This story happened in Dorrego or in Tapalque. Now a flood covers the whole area, but some years ago, during the first term of Perón's government, I believe, or the last of Illia, there was a theater. A small theater, not bigger than a kitchen, whose walls were covered with allegorical frescoes. The mother, the Minotaur, Agamemnon.

Yes, the local women assisted the actors and offered them refreshments. Nothing that these people have not done before. Suárez recited several poems to them. Nothing that he hasn't done before.

Outside, somewhere, a cloud of clothes was floating in the pampas, carried by a capricious wind. Laces, dresses, shoes ... everything ... lost.

The hotel had a room, a yellow room that could be used as a theater. Very few people could enter, but since their audience was already there (for boredom makes people gather), there was no better place for a play.

It is in June when their men slaughter the cows that had already been delivered.

When looking around, he discovered some cow hides in a storehouse. His feverish imagination led him to visualize the whole play, a representation of the *Oresteia.* To be the first to present Aeschylus's *Agamemnon* in Pringles. An epic play with characters in the middle of the pampas. He was the first one to imagine Agamemnon in the middle of the pampas.

To be the first ... is precisely to look for what is already there, in the pampas.

Momo was still sleeping when Martha woke up. He didn't see her walking around a room with mirrors, chandeliers, and useless chairs. He never saw her looking at her face and at her entire body. An entire order of decay.

Perhaps deep in her eyes, she saw her whole existence. A vulgar destiny shaped in decency. It was, perhaps, the first time she saw a cow in front of a mirror.

She was the beef of herself, the flesh, a beef only digestible with more and more wine. Ten years of solitude. Acting for the most part. But acting beyond the scene. Acting for Suárez, acting for Momo, acting for herself. Simply, acting.

She tried to cover up his face with the scarce make-up she found. Then also her hair and her breasts. White patches covering her skin. Pale cow, pure eyes. She asked one of the *matronas* to help her with the corset ... for "she must have a feminine appearance and an absence of tendency to lay on fat. She should be in good flesh but not beefy. Her chest broad and deep, shoulders within, vertebrae and hips prominent and firm, muzzle, large, mouth broad, nostril large and open, head erect, neck slender, her eyes alert and placid, her hips wide apart and level, her back straight, her rump long and wide and level, her skin mellow, her hair ..." (Griffin, *Women and Nature,* 68).

She didn't finish applying the make-up. Instead, she asked for help to put a corset. An enormous corset that constrained her body. Necessity itself. Forcing her to smile. And to cover herself with cow hides.

"Ten years have passed since the strong sons of Atreus
Menelaus and Agamemnon, both alike
Honored by Zeus with throned and sceptred powers
Gathered and manned a thousand Argive ships...." (Aeschylus, *Agamemnon,* 42–44).

When he discovered the cow hides stored in the house, he immediately thought about his own place in the pampas. He didn't follow any particular path of thinking. He let himself be carried by his thoughts. Wandering, almost completely lost, he realized that he was a great actor. Then, he came to blame his lack of success on simple misunderstandings. Essential misunderstandings, indeed. He enjoyed strictly following the lines of his scripts, and rehearsing the plot strict lines, and preparing the material, but he lived in a land that revered improvisation, spontaneity, the contortions of the body, the cruelty of unjustified tortures, and states of trance. Circular stories most of them. Repetitions of repetitions.

He was about to realize that he was in the pampas. A perfect reconciliation. A conflagration. The One. And all that because of the skins! Suddenly, he felt thirsty, but not precisely for truth. He decided to make a turn and follow the paths of the cows. For only they know the paths toward the ponds.

Besides, a title like the *Oresteia* may not say anything to simple folks. A title like *The Return of Zoilo* could summarize, in a sentence, the favorite topics to which every conversation leads. A war, a defeat, the *νόστος*, boredom. The perfect monad. Back at the hotel he talked to Momo and to his woman about all these ideas, but this time he used his new language, that of the continuum. Improvising, contradicting himself, rolling on the floor, and finally crying.

I cannot tell whether she heard a word of the speech or whether she was too busy combing her hair.

Under the circumstances Momo resembled Iphigenia more than Cassandra. He was the daughter of an uncertain, troubled marriage, almost an orphan. No, they had never adopted him. He was the perfect idiot, the one that repeats thoughts, always changing, always distorting the plot. The chorus.

So Agamemnon, rather than retreat,
Endured to offer up his daughter's life
To help a war fought for a faithless wife
And pay the ransom for a storm-bound fleet (Cf. Aeschylus, *Agamemnon*, 148–155).

Let's say, then, that she fell asleep and had an erotic dream..., About Buenos Aires. In the dream, Buenos Aires was finally covered by a flood. The whole town bursting into tears, turning into helpless despair, tears that the make-up could not cover. Tears for her maiden years (Cf. *Agamemnon,* 172–174).

She drank a little just to keep herself awake, but he was the thirsty one. Two or three cups of that wine transformed her into another monster. She resembled a cow more and more. "She is a great cow. She stands in the midst of her own soft flesh, her thighs great wide arches, round columns, her hips wide enough for calving, sturdy, rounded, swaying, stupefied mass, a cradle, a waving field of nipples, her udder brushing the grass, a great cow, who thinks nothing, who waits to be milked, year after year, who delivers up calves, who stands ready for the bull, who is faithful, always there, yielding at the same hour, day after day, that warm substance, the milk white of her eye, staring, trusting, sluggish, bucolic, inert, bovine, mind dozing and dreaming, who lays open her flesh, like a drone, for the use of the world" (*Woman and Nature,* 67).

Her outburst: "Our Argive men had captured Priam's town" (*Agamemnon,* 263).

Momo, like a chorus: "I heard it wrong. I can't believe it!"
Clytemnestra: "Troy is ours! Is that clear speaking?"
Momo: "*Viva la patria!* Death to the savage Unitarians!"

No rule to keep, no order of place, each with their luck (Cf. *Agamemnon,* 333).

Clytemnestra skipped several lines of the script. She replaced them with a dance, with contortions and groans. Finally, she whispered "I sang for joy to hail this victory long ago" (*Agamemnon,* 590). Momo approached her and embraced her, but she covered his mouth with her right, kindly hand. "I will hear all from the king's own lips" (*Agamemnon,* 592).

She sang, joyful … a spontaneous Latin sprang like milk from her very breast …

Beata cujus ubera
Summo repleta munere

Terris alebant unicam
Terrae polique gloriam …

"She is bred for her fat in her milk. The sire is chosen through a measure of the fat in his daughter's milk. That calf whose daughter's milk may be unworthy is eliminated as a sire. (He is approached in a standing position. Two slits are made in the bottom of his scrotum; the testicles are drawn out; the cord of each testicle is broken or severed. The end of the cord is touched with a hot iron. Or the cord is cut with an instrument which crushes the end of the cord as it is cut)" (*Woman and Nature,* 69).

Then she collapsed, her womb seemed to explode. She squeezed her breasts with fury, for she felt the presence of Orestes—the milking machine, the Vacuum—who wants to draw the milk from the teat. Women glanced at her steps, and then began to follow her.

Agamemnon entered in his chariot, followed by another chariot bearing spoils of war and Cassandra. Agamemnon-Zoilo:
First, Tapalque, and your native gods, kindly receive …
The conqueror's greeting on my safe return;
Now for this victory let us give our pious thanksgiving …
Warms without envy to a friend's rancho prosperity …

Then Clytemnestra entered, attended by maids holding a long drape of crimson silk …
Her tears of joy. Her breast, completely dry. Now she is the South, Justice, the very end. "For me—the springing torrents of my tears are all drawn dry, no drop left, and my sleepless eyes are now with weeping may the lamp long lit for your in vain" (Cf. *Agamemnon,* 1887–1990).

In the other chariot, Cassandra-Momo waited for their turn, covered with hide.

Zoilo: "take this girl into the rancho and treat her well."

Clytemnestra enters again. "Now, dearest husband, come, step from your chariot. But do not set to earth, my lord, the conquering silk …" she orders, and she herself spreads the silk before her master's feet; for "Justice herself … shall lead you to a home you never hoped to see" (Cf. *Agamemnon,* 938).

Zoilo, stopping his contortions, yawned: "*Pero, ché* … your speech was longer than my absence!" (Cf. *Agamemnon,* 746).

Yet he stepped on the hides ...

He perceived that an entire chorus of women in the audience were echoing her voice, imitating her gestures, sucking their breasts, kicking, screaming.... "The cow may begin to show bad habits. She may suck her own teats or those of other cows. Secure a metal anti-sucking device and fasten it in the cow's nostril, or put a halter on her, and on the halter strap a nose strap covered by another strap through which sharp nails point outward. She may kick: secure a set of hobbles and fasten these on her legs" (*Woman and Nature,* 70).

It was then, and not before, that Agamemnon understood his South American destiny. In their cow eyes, he was Zoilo, the one who returns as many ... and he understood that it was time for him to celebrate, to slaughter *that* cow, to breed Cassandra, to live his life as a recluse in the pampas, supreme rancho.

Momo recited his part by heart. Without omissions, without mistakes. Almost merciless, as is his heart. In his infinite servitude, in his idiotic mind he found the continuum, if not himself. He / She, Cassandra—Momo whispered:

"Apollo ... leader of journeys, my destroyer ...
you have led me so far, to strike me once again!
A heart obsesses with indifference now ...
And here! ... And there!
Silver dagger, betray me, and you
... come friends and drink ...
The one who holds it ...
Woke up next to you ...
Now she strikes! Now he lies on the ground.
May your blood reach the muddy shores of Lethe."

Some from the audience, loud-mouthed, asked him for the meaning of these words. He merely replied: "I say Agamemnon shall lie dead before your eyes" (1213).

From behind a white sheet hung for the occasion, they glanced at the scene. He screamed: "*Pero ché....*"

No one screamed.

Their voices had changed. They began to moo. In the middle of that confusion Clytemnestra restored the law in the pampas.

"That which is cruel
cannot be approved of censored, for these are one, if not the same …
There he lies, the one I love,
Neither in the marshes, nor behind the mountains …
Kind hands received him, loud-mouthed truth,
And Justice as well" (Cf. *Agamemnon,* 1372).

Her hands tied down the sheet covering the scene, and Zoilo, supreme Agamemnon, lay dead on the ground, wrapped in a voluminous cow hide. Momo lay there as well.

Outside, a crowd of men was beating on the doors of the hotel. The loud bellowing and bawling scared them away. Clytemnestra said what has already been said: "We are the cows. With our large brown eyes and our soft fur there was once something called beauty that we were part of. It is this we remember when we bellow. When we stand still and gaze at you. Our noses were wet, we know that, we know we once nuzzled you as you pulled with your hands on us, as the milk rushed warm against our bellies, rushed through us, sighing within us as it flowed, or as the tongues of our calves licked our teats and our skin shivered, and the calf's mouth closed over us, and we remembered the shaking body as it slid from our thighs, and we licked it, amazing and new, over its skin, licked it clean, and now it licks us, nuzzles us, its brown eye staring into our eye, skin and fur, one against the other, the one and the same, one shiver, and one sigh, one warm rush of sweetness in the mouth, and the soft bodies, growing nightly, soft against ours, to run with us, we remember that once we stood together in the fields, we remember what we were then, what then to be part, to be part of our beauty" (*Woman and Nature,* 72).

Then both Agamemnon and Momo stand up and joined her singing:
"They may howl, we may roll onto our backs
they may slaughter, if we are the dagger …"
la casa está en orden! (1707–1708).

The doors suddenly opened, and they disbanded and wandered off.

Somewhere in the pampas a cloud of clothes was floating. Carried by a capricious wind. Laces, dresses, shoes …

Everything … lost.

Images of Cruelty

The display of cruelty we have performed reveals the excess in the events that took place in the house of Peleus, and that this excess is not to be interpreted in terms of a historizing within which "history likes to repeat itself." This likening, this taste for repetition is, rather, *κόρος,* takes more than its place, being otherwise. The events that took place in the house of Suárez unfolded themselves in monstrous recollections, echoes, images that had been taking place in Argos in advance.

If we understand Borges's observations on history in relation to this last sense, we see that cruelty finds its expression in a chorus that in addition to carrying the characters, displays the way actions exceed actions. This is the way that mimesis is to be understood. Thus, the tragedy itself is exceeded by the tragic. The default is to exceed its images. But if this is the case, why do certain images seem to persist? How do these images make room? What is the way of historizing the ontology that these images display?

One might hear it said that the view of place underlying this taking place of being in the pampas resembles the one advanced by the Platonic notion of *ὕλε* or *χώρα*: an undefined something waiting to be filled by images—a vessel, a receptacle for being—and therefore, of being as something that by its definition exceeds that *place.* The pampas within this interpretation appears as a "mere" place, "mere" setting for whatever events or phenomena happen to occur within it. And indeed, as if there is nothing arbitrary in these events. This is manifest in the political problem of the pampas—of the discontinuity of the territory. The continuum of being is displayed in forms, ideas, and images that unfold as a piece of cloth, depreciated coins, and signs. But these unfoldings show that the pampas, as *place,* stretch themselves to go beyond the boundaries of territory. Isn't this displayed, for example, in the coinage minted before the default, in the depreciation, in the circumspect acceptance that alteration, fluctuation, is an aesthetic phenomenon exceeding any economic interest? Extension, then, mimics *place*.

Being makes manifest that *κόρος*, excess, *ἄπειρον*, are imperatives upon beings. The aesthetic unconcealment of being in the pampas suggests this imperative of being otherwise by advancing the mimesis between place and extension. This aesthetics of excess is what images, fashion, theater, coinage, and signs have to make manifest. It is a refusal to engage in the development of any particular philosophical anthropology of characters as a forestructure telling us what it is to be Huiliche, or to be Argentinean. The *in* in such forestructures is excessive, takes more and less place than itself.

Artaud's theater of cruelty offers this ontological insight in which the forestructure is conceived as a "perpetual play of mirrors passing from color to gesture and from cry to movement [that] leads us unceasingly along roads rough and difficult for the mind, plunges us into that state of uncertainty and ineffable anguish which is the characteristic of poetry" (Artaud, *The Theater and Its Double*, 63). Indeed, what is the theater of cruelty in the pampas? Who is Artaud in the pampas? How does the theater unfold itself in this territory? Ultimately, how can someone justify the fact that in asking about being in the pampas a writer might be compelled to invent some kind of theater play? What understanding are we supposed to take from these many signs? These concerns are to remain unanswered until we have made explicit what we have called the "exhibition" and "display" of being.

First, we must focus our attention on certain paths that temporal ontology has followed in the task of thematizing poetics itself. To poetize—in both a general and a Greek sense—is to "bring forth." As Heidegger has shown, this definition is already a hyperinflated one. What is to be brought up is being itself, but once poetics has been subsumed to the question of the temporality of being, poetics comes forth as an analytic of the plot and of its poetic "effects." The question of *κάθαρσις*, according to Aristotle, is a question that concerns not only the "expurgation" of certain emotions, but first and foremost the motions of the soul and the *κόρος* or excesses that the soul is subject to, which have to be bounded by means of cathartic effects. What is present in tongue and in signs that has entailed that catharsis itself to be thematized in terms of diction rather than in terms of actions, of movement? One may find this difficulty given in advance in the *Physics:* "time then is not movement, but that by which movement can be numerically estimated" (Aristotle, *Physics*, IV, 219b5–7). But what if their motions exceed themselves? The characters may run away, roll on the floor, be taken by convulsions and contortions, they may be inclined to commit murder. Isn't this atrocious? If the plot is written in advance, and the character's names are given after, temporality ensures a bounded, political continuum between the plot and the performance of the play. Indeed, this submission within temporality displays the cutting off of being from what is in being.

It is only when the question of displaying being is brought forth, that the attempt to conceptualize ontology in purely temporal terms comes into question. This is precisely what happens in Artaud's reflections on theater. When Artaud advocates a theater of cruelty, he traces it back to the question of being in its primary, Eleatic sense, where being is understood as a question of *place*. The theater is a *place* to display the ways motion and stillness exceed their being. Artaud finds it particularly disgraceful that Western theater became only a theater of words, and unlike Aristotle, he is concerned with the "physics of the absolute gesture" (*The Theater and Its Double,* 62). Doesn't this sound like a concern regarding *κόρος*? Doesn't it imply a review of the way that the notion of *ἄπειρον* has been circumspectively thematized by a temporal ontology that measures the events in terms of before and after? "To change the role of speech in theater," says Artaud, "is to make use of it in a concrete and spatial sense" (*The Theater and Its Double,* 73). Is this use given in advance in speech itself? But if this is the case, then beings exceed their very taking place. A body in motion is "a solid object, one which overturns and disturbs things, in the air first of all, then in an infinitely more mysterious and secret domain *but one that admits extension*" (*The Theater and Its Double,* 72). Without thematizing this taking place of being by means of displaying, "it will not be very difficult to identify this secret but extended domain with that of formal anarchy on the one hand but also with that of continuous formal creation on the other" (*The Theater and Its Double,* 72).

Artaud follows the spatial path of what is in being without falling back into some kind of "temporal" difficulty in stating a metaphysical theater, in recovering the question of being as a question of "place": "the theater's purpose with every possibility of formal and extended manifestation gives rise to the idea of a certain poetry in space which itself is taken for sorcery" (*The Theater and Its Double,* 72).

The displays brought forth by the theater of cruelty must be conceived as a certain historizing of ontology; one that follows the goddess's precept: "because the same things that you see with your eyes are in being," in a way that ontology "must give us everything that is in crime, love, war, or madness, if it wants to recover its necessity" (*The Theater and Its Double,* 85). In this mimesis we "shall try to concentrate, around famous personages, atrocious crimes, superhuman devotions, a drama which, without resorting to the defunct images of the old myths, shows that it can extract the forces which struggle within them" (*The Theater and Its Double,* 85). Wasn't this the very way that "Hellenist" thinkers conceived the Eleatic fragments as taking place?

Thus, the manifesto on cruelty is to be conceived beyond its theatrical boundaries as a manifesto on the question of being. Ontology—rather than theater—is to be thematized "through its physical aspect, since it requires *expression in space*" (*The Theater and Its Double,* 89) in such a way that it exceeds itself, and its inquiry "cannot be defined except by its possibilites for dynamic expression in space" (*The Theater and Its Double,* 89).

Ontology unfolds *κόρος* beyond the concern for insolence. If Artaud agrees with Aristotle that in any display of being "it is not a matter of boring the public," their "solutions" have been radically different, and in the way such difference is to be conceived as excess, as granting or not granting the taking place of being in the pampas. Parting ways with Aristotle, ontology, the thematizing of what happens here and there, becomes a spectacle that unfolds a continuum of physical and objective elements, perceptible to all, that always includes "cries, groans, apparitions, surprises, theatricalities of all kinds, magic beauty of costumes taken from certain ritual models; resplendent lighting, incantational beauty of voices, the charms of harmony, rare notes of music, colors of objects, physical rhythm of movements ... concrete appearances of new and surprising objects, masks, effigies yards high" (*The Theater and Its Double,* 93). And indeed, in a reverse way, ontology's place, the *mise en scène,* is the "point of departure for all theatrical creation" (*The Theater and Its Double,* 94). Gestures, images, signs, clothes become evocative, *ἄπειρον*, and it is in this sense that the continuum must be understood. The fashionable nature of theatrical costumes, for instance, is a phenomenon that unfolds being in its spatial sense, and it reveals the diffusion, the uncontrolled, unrestricted celebration of forms that exceed their own place of representation and go beyond the settings of the theater and take place on any street, in the pampas themselves.

This taking place of being in the pampas asks us to "abolish the stage and the auditorium and replace them by a single site, without partition or barrier of any kind, which will become the theater of action" (*The Theater and Its Double*, 96). In Artaud's view actions, which imitate action itself, must come from every corner of the room. The actors are to move, and the audience may follow them, "some seeking prophecies, while others, for many a day stabbed by grievous pains, beg to hear the word that heals all manner of illness" (Empedocles, *Fragments*, 112). The politics of the continuum in the pampas is finally explicit in the imperative of not performing an ontological play, but rather to "make attempts at direct staging, around themes, facts, or known works."

Against the temporal "not yet taking place" that we have made explicit in being in the pampas, Artaud counterposes a taking place that is given in advance by "themes that will be cosmic, universal and interpreted according to the most ancient texts drawn from old Mexican, Hindu, Judaic, and Iranian cosmogonies, etc." (*The Theater and Its Double*, 123). In this shift from the question of the plot, and from diction to action, "place" extends itself beyond itself. It is only in a temporal historizing of ontology that the question concerning the locality of certain traditions could ever take place, as a certain communitarianism closes over itself, an experience that no culture has ever known except in terms of excess. Ontology moves through the pampas as a certain taking place that exceeds its very place. Its being a stage must display what is already taking place: gods, heroes, monsters, natural and cosmic forces "interpreted according to images from the most ancient sacred texts and old cosmogonies" (*The Theater and Its Double*, 123).

Images, *εἴδη*, give in advance this unfolding of being in the pampas. We know, by the testimony of Pausanias, that the ancient Greeks used to learn by going into the presence of the gods. The gods unconcealed being by speaking and displaying images, which were later written down as truth, and indeed, as what exceeds truth. (Cf. Pausanias, *Description of Greece*, II, 348–355).

Before going to Trophonio's, the initiated bathed themselves in the waters of *Λήθη*. *Λήθη* appears already in closeness to *ἀλήθεια*, to un-concealment. Truth, we know, is an un-concealment of what is in being. But as Heidegger points out, *Λήθη* is not concealment as hiding, but a certain "making room" that has to do with an understanding of the political-hygienic as calling into place what is to be forgotten, for forgetting and knowing take a certain place (Heidegger, *Parmenides*, 131–163). The initiates are bathed in the waters of *Λήθη*, in the waters of a certain kind of oblivion, one that refers to a being that is not in continuity. After that, the initiates are brought to the waters of *Μνεμοσύνη*, and bathed again, completing the "making room" for being to take place as otherwise, as *ἄπειρον*, as truth. The descent into the cave and the seating of the initiated on the chair of memory, are the politics of excess. The goddess who oriented Parmenides also displayed the many images of what is in being as taking place and as exceeding their place. Images are not indexicals, they point toward being. An indexical—if such a thing is possible—means that at a certain time it localizes a precise object. In doing so, indexicals take over a notion of temporality: something should be in its own place and never exceed its own place. But images exceed themselves and embrace themselves in the continuum of being.

In Plato's *Republic* we find another reference to the procedure of learning by looking at images. His thematizing of being as something to be displayed is not well understood. Scholars think of this as an allegory, but by allegory they do not mean "to refer to something else" in terms of taking place elsewhere, but in the sense of a story that may mean something else that we can not yet fully grasp; something that cannot be fully grasped at this moment but at some other moment it will be fully known. In their analysis of Plato's allegory of the cave they seem to focus their attention on a temporal question with regard to knowledge, rather than an ontological unfolding with regard to being itself and its taking place in images.

Temporalizing interpretations of Plato's story insist on the fact that the images of the cave are false, mere representations of what is in being by means of artificial objects contrasting with the real world of ideas that unfold themselves beyond the boundaries of the cave. What the initiated learn by looking at images and listening is that being exceeds itself and that the being of beings exceeds its place. This is what is intended by displaying "images of implements of all kinds that rise above the wall, and human images and shapes of animals ... some speaking and others silent." Why are these so often thematized as nothing more than mere "shadows of artificial objects" (Plato, *The Republic*, 515c)?

OLIVIERI

For the thinkers of the Eleatic school—particularly Parmenides and Empedocles—truth is characterized poetically. Besides its "crypticality" (Clement, *Miscellanies,* V. 2, 15), Parmenides' poem was, for the Hellenistic thinkers, a bringing forth of truth in a way that the locus of truth—its being—is never exclusively *ὅρος,* assertions, or subordinated to the notion of chronology.

Heidegger ventured the hypothesis that humans dwell poetically. *Ποίησις* exceeds the doings of poets, and becomes that which denotes the ontological way that humanity has for dwelling in being. It is in this sense that early Greeks found Parmenides' poem a place of truth. Instead of a philosophically distorted or impure thinking, they conceived it as the product of rigorous or even cruel intellectuality, for it was a product of certain cruel exercises over Parmenides himself—one that takes the laugh from the body, that compelled him to write tablets afterward, also that provided a number of forces to throw one against the other, to bitterly argue, delete, amend, come to forget the events that took place in Velia, and in other places otherwise. We defined this turmoil as ontology, but the phenomenon itself has not quite been reconstructed or even understood.

Parmenides' poem has succeeded in its metric attempt to unconceal truth for as long as it has "survived" as fragments. Its fragmentary character makes us even more aware of unfolding truth, as long as it took place. Diogenes Laertius reports that Parmenides "commits his doctrine to verse" (Diogenes Laertius, *Life of Eminent Philosophers,* IX, 21–3), in a style that his admirer Empedocles imitated (*Life of Eminent Philosophers,* VIII, 55). Somewhere else, in Greece, the Suda adds "and some other things in prose, which Plato mentions" (Diels-Kranz, *Die Fragmente der Vorsokratiker,* A2). Furthermore, in Chaeronea, under the sun of the beach, Plutarch found Parmenides at fault "for his versification," no less than Sophocles for his unevenness (Cf. *Vorsokratiker*, A15). Proclus vituperated his "unclear poetic style" (Cf. *Vorsokratiker*, A18) but admits the possibility that Parmenides may prove these things "both through steadfast heart of persuasive truth / and the beliefs of mortals, in which there is no true trust" (Parmenides, Fragment 1). Yet he prefigured the objection that Parmenides account was "yet although obliged, because of the poetic form itself, to use the metaphorical terms, figures, and turns of phrases, he nevertheless embraced the most unbecoming, dry, and austere form of expression" to the point that his verses may be "read more like prose than poetry" (Cf. *Vorsokratiker*, A18). In Rome, Simplicius taught and impugned its enigmatic character (Cf. *Vorsokratiker*, A19).

Needless to say, in its taking place beyond Velia, the poem was accessible for further retellings, by thinkers who interpreted, added to it, came to forget, forged, reflected, divulged it with a certain joy, painted, rectified, impugned, secretly kept it in urns, used it for an astronomical demonstration, preserved it in codices, changed its very words, lost it to fire, sang, inverted, took it as an emblem, translated, pondered it with disdain, turned unrecognizable, tolerated, represented it in a theatre play, used it to prove their own doctrine.... But these spreadings, retellings of truth, differ from Aristotle's distinction between *φυσικόι* and *φυσιολόγοι*; a distinction between one who is engaging in telling and retelling stories and one who investigates the nature of what is; and from that other distinction between *μῦθος* and *ποίησις*. These ensured that truth is dwelling, placed within an assertion.

Borges used to say that history likes to repeat itself perhaps as a way to express how events took place, and as in a theater company, they are to repeat its play in other places and other circumstances. The murderous events of New Rome show this conflict between those who procured hexameter as a way of conveying truth, and the subsequent events, those that led to the publishing of a newspaper in the pampas (*La Legione Agricola*) and to the study of meteorology (Cf. Crespi Valls, *Primer Centenario de la Legión Agrícola Militar*, 54–57). Even in this change of method, the soldiers managed to remain on the way without going straightway toward the unconcealment of the murder; and this is shown in the excess of versions, rumors, retellings of Olivieri's crime. This succession of versions did not distort the events by dissembling, in a sense of ψευδής, but in a sense of satiety, κόρος, one that leads to insolence.

"Olivieri," one version affirms,

> requested to dig a cave in New Rome, a cave whose vestiges still remain, where he confined for days or for weeks as a disciplinary punishment those individuals who did not behave accordingly, were vicious, etc. Several days before his death, someone let him know—through an anonymous letter or by other means—that the individuals complained about those punishments and that they were organizing a plot; but he, in his typical vehement gesture, said aloud for any one to hear him: I will shoot you if you keep annoying me, refusing to fulfill your duties, and not behaving with the due decorum (Crespi Valls, *Primer Centenario*, 95).

These assertions both reveal and conceal the events that took place, for we do not understand the method, the procedures by which Olivieri attempted to find truth, the *compostura*, the decorum, the composure, the neatness due in the pampas. Is he referring to the "hanging askew," the cruelty of lowering a man into a cave until, being paralyzed by what is in being, he may be able to unconceal truth? Other versions, no less faithfully say "according to some soldiers, there is mysterious bird that lives in the well, a bird that was caught and confined in a room but escaped without opening the door. There are some who believe that this bird is the soul of the priest; I saw it, and I can assure that it is a hawk" (Cf. *Primer Centenario*, 98).

Olivieri's conviction that those events must take place, that any soldier must experience the κατάβασις that leads to the unconcealment of being ran against the forces of the soldiers. The conspiracy, indeed, is not completely justified, for there were no boundaries that enslaved the soldiers in the boundless pampas. Their "standing in reserve" comes from the understanding advanced in the phrase "to be on tenterhooks" (*estaban en capilla*), which not only denotes the futility of boundaries in the pampas, but also the inner cruelty surrounding its freedom: it compels beings to double themselves, to be otherwise than they are. What else is revealed by the fashionable uniforms in the middle of the pampas? Again, "what is called New Rome is a camp on a corner of the stream, without moat, where there are camped ten national guards and twenty Indians who sleep in the open air, without tents nor ranch that may shelter them from rain. Those people are, one may say, on tenterhooks: if the Indians want to attack, none of them will escape" (*Primer Centenario*, 98).

To be on tenterhooks, *estar en capilla,* already denotes a certain standing in reserve, and at the same time, being afraid of something imminent that may take place, something that is already known in advance but whose form or reason is not clearly expressed. This silence echoes that of the captive herself: "when something's true, you know it the first time you hear it" (Borges, *Collected Fictions,* 448), but at the same time suggests the enframing of images that are to persist in whatever takes place in the pampas, technology itself.

Chronology adds nothing to this assertion, for the difficulty resides in the understanding of this fear, the direction, the locus, the way from which the enemy advances. Temporal interpretations of the *pozo* as a well seem to focus on the idea that its use was that of a water reservoir, a reservoir on the top of a hill for a fortress without walls and with a stream already there, down the hill, providing water the whole year around.

If Olivieri's intentions were to imprison his troops in a cave until the orderliness of the kind of truth that could be written in tablets was revealed, then how are we to understand the fact that "later he [the *κοῦρος*] comes to his senses no better than before?" Indeed, what ensures such understanding is the fact that he can laugh again (Pausanias, *Description of Greece,* 395) by reaching a certain understanding that is still to be unconcealed, written in the tablets. Is this an understanding of technology itself, of enframing, of being as taking place in the pampas, of the need for doubling the bodies?

Traveler's journals report this going down into the cave, but only in terms of a terrifying experience: "He put his feet on the ground of the pit; then we heard his screams asking us to lift him. We did so without delay, and when we got him up, we saw him pale like a cadaver and breathing heavily. After some seconds in which he inhaled air with all the strength of his lungs, he told us that he almost suffocated himself down there, because in that excavation one could not breathe air, but carbonic acid...." (Crespi Valls, *Primer Centenario,* 100). But they also suggest the excess, that something else was intended by the digging: "When he came out to the surface, he was livid and unconscious. Only some minutes after he started to regain consciousness. We should note that the well where this *señor* descended is no more than 18 feet deep, and no less than 4½ feet in diameter, so that there is plenty of fresh air, and there is no reason to think that the air is not fresh at the bottom...." (*Primer Centenario*, 101).

Olivieri's procedures offer a reversal of that posted by Heidegger for understanding confirmation. Instead of someone "with his back turned to the wall (making) the true assertion that 'the picture on the wall is hanging askew,'" Olivieri is hanging men askew to compel them to look at pictures, "upside down" in the already "upside down" pampas (Cf. Aira, *The Hare*). What is to be perceived and confirmed, indeed, is what lies beyond, what exceeds the images: the *ἄπειρον* character of the pampas. All the doublings before this step go into that direction: the uniforms, the mintage machine, the many tablets that Olivieri brought from Buenos Aires.

Eleatic thinkers, for whom Aristotle expressed contempt, characterized being as *ἕν καὶ ἀκίνητον τὸ πᾶν εἶναι φασι, καὶ ἄπειρον ἔνιον. Τὸ γὰρ πέρας περαίνειν ἄν πρός τὸ κενόν,* "they assert that the universe is one and immovable; some add that it is infinite as well, for the limit would be a limit against the void" (Aristotle, *De Generatione et Corruptione*, 325a15–7); and with regard to any inquiry concerning truth *εἰ γὰρ ἄπειρον ειε, ειε ἄν. Ει γὰρ δύο ειε, ουκ ἄν δυναιτο απεια ναι, ἀλλ' εφοι ἄν πεῖρατα πρός ἀλλελε,* "for if it were *apeiron*, it would be one; for if it were two, the two could not be *apeiron*, but would be limited by one another" (Simplicius, *Commentary on Aristotle's De Caelo* 557, 16). Eleatic philosophy, indeed, made explicit that being is, and is to be conceived as limitless on every side.

This understanding of being, and perhaps no other, carried Olivieri to start an expedition to the pampas by ship and to establish New Rome as a place for seeking truth. The maps of the construction site that were preserved show that water was abundant near the unfortified fortress. A stream passed by, and from the hill it could be seen as two rivers. On top of the hill, there was a cave, 30 feet deep. There were paths leading from the river to the top. This particular arrangement can be better understood by carefully reading the testimony of Pausanias about the oracle of Throponios.

We may interpret Olivieri's attempt as a certain disclosure of truth by means of an oracle. He had decided in advance that his troops must visit the underworld. He confined some of these men in the rancho of Good Fortune for a certain number of days. These wretched were then taken to the stream where they were strictly purified. Olivieri might offer an *asado* or sardines as a sacrifice, and as a way of spreading more rumors around the event. He might mention Persephone, the monthly salary, the cards, a hare. Then, he interpreted the many signs remaining in the leftovers, and foretold what was awaiting the men going down. How could they be sure that the goddess would receive them kindly and graciously? What is kindness in the middle of the pampas? Can anyone go down in true hope? Is the default to be unconcealed before going down? Well, then, they were taken at night to the *Sauce Chico* stream, where they were painted, anointed with vinegar and salt, and washed. A whole chorus follows these men who are going down, spreading rumors, gossiping. They drink the water of the Forgetfulness, to forget everything in their mind until then. Then they walk down the stream and drink again, but this time only the water of Memory by which they hope to remember the images they might see in their descent. Then they mint some bills following their own design. After this, they go to the oracle wearing their uniform, their medals, and no socks but heavy local boots. The oracle is on top of a hill. It is a chasm in the earth, whose depths are unknown. The chasm is closed by doors. Olivieri provides a light, narrow ladder to those who descend. They go down bringing some of the bills they have minted. Now, in the well, they are taught the future. Some of them hear it, some of them see it also. Those who did not observe the ritual seem to stay longer, but all of them return. When a man comes up from the goddess's oracle the chorus seats him on a chair brought from France called the throne of Memory. Everyone asks him what he saw and discovered. They call this "giving laws." Once they have satisfied their curiosity with him, they carry him to the rancho of Good Spirit and Fortune. The descendant is usually possessed with terror and he complains about the bureaucracy, the State, and fashion. When he finally comes to his senses, he is as wretched as before, but now he starts to laugh very loud. Everyone who goes down to the goddess's oracle is supposed to write a treatise on *ποίησις* in the pampas.

This interpretation of the events of New Rome exhibits the character of *ἀλήθεια* not only as unconcealment, but primordially as that which is does not go away by the wash of *Λήθη*. Heidegger pointed out that *ἀ-λήθεια* means that truth is not drenched, "washed away" by *Λήθη*. Such evidence, then, gives clues for a definition of truth as that which exceeds itself, and emerges from the water of forgetting.

In his inquiry concerning the character of Lethe, Heidegger refers to this as "emerging" and he relates it to a certain "coming forth" of being in such a way that he contraposes *λήθη* and *φύσις*. "Lethe does not admit any *phuein*, any emerging and coming forth" (Heidegger, *Parmenides*, 120). Investment in infrastructure displays how the nature of bureaucracy is that of withdrawing and concealing, for it does not allow anything to emerge, and hence it sets itself against all coming forth. On the contrary, the continuum is the place where the uncanny dwells. Suspicious, murderous attempts, retellings, are ways of moving forth and emerging from the spring or stream of *Λήθη*. Indeed, no one can emerge without being soaked in *Λήθη*. Further, the body of the one who descends to the goddess is soaked in advance: drenched, bringing cakes, and going from darkness into darkness.

The ambiguity and difficulty in understanding the events of New Rome resides, perhaps, in the ambiguous character of the stream, for the stream of *Λήθη* and that of *Μνεμοσύνη* are one and the same, and in the way that they are not: different locations, different pyres, different procedures to be followed in each of them. Indeed, "the place of Lethe is that 'where' in which the uncanny dwells in a peculiar exclusivity," but in its murderous excess "the field of Lethe is, in preeminent sense, 'demonic'" (Heidegger, *Parmenides*, 119). The "carefree" character of the inquiry contrasts with the careful character of any method. Not only because the waters of Λήθη know nothing of care, but also because the one who steps in the stream is already engaged in a *μέθοδος*. After the murder of Olivieri, his soldiers recollected that something went wrong in his attempt, that he "*metió la pata*" (which somehow suffices as an explanation, as long as the reasons seem to go away as in the waters of the river itself) (Cf. Crespi Valls, *Primer Centenario de la Legión Agrícola Militar*, 54–57).

Invariably, retelling recollects the inner cruelty of Olivieri, the sententious "I will confine all of you in the cave," his gestures demanding that the soldiers wear full uniforms in the pampas, his cursing *Razzi di cani!*, the "demonic" in his seeking truth by means of *κόρος*, by doubling the bodies.

Fashion

When we trace the unfolding of being back to the goddess's speech and to Eleatic philosophy, and we emphasize that such unfolding was made by means of images, of course we are not claiming that the images we recover and see are the very same ones Parmenides saw. This means, then, that there is an issue still at bay—that concerning the relation between the images and the fragments of Parmenides. If images exceed themselves, and the goddess displays those images as a continuum of what is in being, then it seems that signs (and the fragments) should present the same attribute. But this runs against traditional accounts that rely on a purely temporal understanding of being, and affirms that signs should extend their reference toward a certain object, and in so doing, the model that is preferred is that of the univocal reference, of indexicals, of proper names.

We have heard, for instance, temporal ontology read Plato's *Cratylus* as an aporetic dialogue that clashes or confronts the Heraclitean or Eleatic accounts on the nature of signs. Plato, it is said, remains indecisive with regard to those two views, and never quite overcomes this difficulty in his later works. We should be aware that this interpretation relies on a certain understanding of time, for referentiality depends on the divisibility of time in a succession of "divisible nows" that may be a continuum, and ensures that the named being remains in its place without exceeding its own place. When Plato posits Parmenides in Athens he is already addressing the issue of names as they may exceed themselves to address, evoke, lead toward what is otherwise than a certain "object," and otherwise to themselves.

Plato, indeed, puts into question the assumption that signs (*ὄνομα*) can be rendered within a restricted temporal framework, within the boundaries of how to "use names at different times." He uses both Heraclitean and Parmenidean accounts to display that signs always name beyond a certain point or limited place. To understand this principle, we need to pay attention to his demand for motion, "you do not seem to note how I rush along outside the racecourse, when I get on smooth ground" (Plato, *Cratylus,* 414b), to understand his critique of temporality. Temporality demands that when we give signs, we must apply the same sign "whether once or many times ... to nothing else [than that thing], and [naming] nothing else, than that of which it is the name" (Plato, *Parmenides,* 147e). This implies that a sign partakes of time "at one time and does not partake at another; for that is the only way in which it can partake and not partake of the same thing" (Plato, *Parmenides,* 155e). It is because names exceed their references that they can name beyond a certain place.

Thus signs "indicate" as long as their "pointing" exceeds any place. This is the case not because they mean to look toward a certain direction, but because they are referring to place as a continuum between places themselves, and as long as a certain motion also takes place in being. This is made explicit by the etymologies that Plato offers. These etymologies display how signs exceed their pointing by exceeding their meaning. Again, the excess of etymologies grants signs the unfolding of beings. It is this excess that confuses us so much when we read *Cratylus,* for in our interpretations we are always tempted to advance the question of referentiality that derives from a certain way of temporalizing the history of ontology.

Historically ontology has asked whether a certain name is to be attached to a certain object that is "in the succession of nows," and how it is possible for names to name a particular object or event within alteration and motion. The perfect example of this theory is applied to proper names. Plato indicates that any such sign can only name while being in circulation, depreciation, and inflation; that in any case, there must be something in a sign that makes it exceed itself, and makes it point at, or even unconceals a certain being.

If scholars are bothered by these bizarre etymologies, and by the fact that Socrates compares himself with a horse in a race, perhaps it is because they ask for signs to have bounded meanings. The proliferation of etymologies that Plato provides are by no means arbitrary: they show that names "make room" for them, and that it is only by means of such an excess that names can grasp the reality of being.

Etymology, then, becomes ontology; for it manifests itself as a proliferation and abundance of meaning that is inexhaustible. Signs always show an excess of accessibility, for as long as they are in circulation, and they are "running," they exceed themselves and relate to other things in multiple, *ἄπειρον* relations. It is only by means of motion, by means of a cruel doubling of oneself, that this inexhaustible character of signs can be displayed. Why, then, do we insist on pointing out as frivolous this *κόρος* character of signs? Why do we demand that signs name what is ready at hand? What is primordial about this "getting established" of signs?

Such a reductive temporal ontology might be tempted to contrast the "seriousness" of signs with the frivolous, ambiguous, and lavish character of fashion. But why? Can we be sure that signs do not offer the very same notions? That signs themselves are not just as ambiguous as fashion or that fashion is not as "serious" as signs? The difficulty we discover in making such comparisons has to do with the fact that fashion is by no means an entirely temporal phenomenon, but one that has to do with the display of being as extension, as taking place and exceeding itself. Further, fashion displays how ontology takes place and exceeds its own place by means of gossip, further retelling, by inquiring what it is to wear such and such a brand in the pampas or elsewhere.

The phonetic change in Plato, it might be said, cannot be compared with fashion, for in making such a comparison we must know in advance what changes take place at a certain moment with regard to the next one, and this is precisely what fashion does not bring forth without ambiguity and lavishness. "We know only that the changes in fashion depend on laws of imitation, which are the concerns of the psychologist" (Saussure, *Course in General Linguistics*, 151). Why does ontology leave fashion—the way one displays the *more* than one is—aside in its inquiry with regard to signs? Are we sure that signs do not comport as fashion, that the movements of signs do not "depend on laws of imitation" as well? Indeed, Saussure seems to be aware that temporality bounds itself in inquiring into the meaning of signs. "But where is the starting point of imitation?" asks Saussure, "That is the mystery, in phonetic changes as well as in changes in fashion" (*Course in General Linguistics*, 151).

How change takes place in fashion is a question that cannot be answered within the parameters of chronology because what takes place is a change that exceeds time and place, that is, an imitation that takes place and exceeds both itself and its own place.

Fashion falls within the temporal character of beings in a way that precedes time and compels bodies to move within time. If the "shallow" being of fashion must have some meaning, it should be within the reign of frivolity (Cf. Craik, *The Face of Fashion*, 204–225). And indeed, the pampas already offers us this superficial and frivolous characteristic since, to a certain extent, the pampas is nothing other than shallow planes and surfaces. To think being in the pampas is, necessarily, to acknowledge the excessive nature of the frivolous and superficial. Fashion always already displays this phenomenon for understanding and interpretation.

Thinking again of Saussure, it is still historically curious that at the same time he problematized signs in terms of depreciation, he fell back from his account of linguistic change into such a notion of temporality. Why did he prioritize temporality over the taking place of signs? What was the politics of signs behind his own account?

If signs are "radically powerless" against the hyperinflated turmoil of being, against its taking place, and its shiftings, is it because of the politics that signs display: that the discontinuity of the territory is to be manifested and overcome by the shifting that occurs in the relation between the signified and the signifier? This is its arbitrariness and its tendency toward *κόρος*. In dealing with the problem of the discontinuity of the territory we might be compelled to construct a whole logic of continuities, and "this had to be borne in mind when even the most trifling event took place" (Aira, *The Hare*, 33). Aira made explicit that alteration is the product of this continuum: "The Mapuches were constantly creating continuities, and so adept were they at this that they no longer even needed to employ visible or virtual connections, but simply used the continuity itself to perform that function" (*The Hare*, 33).

The sign then is similar to fashion with regard to alteration: it is adapted to exceed the means and the ends pursued. The arbitrariness of fashion reveals that signs exercise cruelty over the human body and compel it to double itself, to be otherwise than itself. Furthermore, like fashion, a sign always exhibits this tendency beyond its natural frontiers by means of circulation, of retellings and ponderings of its value here or there.

Within the boundaries of a temporal ontology, the way the relation between fashion and being might be theorized can be further understood by looking at the way being has been rendered as opposed to *tener* (to have). The expression "es más importante ser que tener" not only repeats a topic that has taking place since Thomas Aquinas' distinction between "*quiditas*" and "*entitas*," and whose accomplished form is to be found in Suárez's *Disputationes*, but it also contrives and gives shape to the relation between fashion and being.

For the most part, the distinction between *tener* and *ser* is expressed by being spoken out, retold, and it has always been expressed this way: being exceeds the having of things, possessions of any kind (to have a car, to be a successful entrepreneur, to have children and populate the empty pampas) ("*tener* auto," "*tener* éxito," "*tener* hijos"). One may notice that a certain understanding of the boundaries of being already underlies what has been spoken. Possession is vituperated, as much as *ambición* is scorned. In this sense, what is emphasized is that one must learn how to resign, to leave behind, to be less than oneself. In such a distinction between *ser* and *tener*, being is spoken as if atemporal, definitive, unchangeable, beyond any material possession, and beyond any "change of season" (Cf. Kusch, *América Profunda*, III, "Sabiduría de América," 179–2540.

Indeed, this understanding is a way of interpreting being that can only claim evidence as long as being is not taking place yet, or taking place without exceeding its limits. It is easy to see that to think this phenomenon in terms of *Dasein* already implies the fully manifest presence of bodies, bodies that already exceed the phenomenological "wearing something." In other words, a certain aesthetic is already presupposed in this denial of being: blue-jeans, black or blue plain t-shirts almost without inscriptions (Guevara's feminine head, a red star, are perhaps ways of resisting this unfashionable move). This image, which in any case is excessive, *ἄπειρον*, controls and distributes any unfolding or even understanding of fashion in the pampas, by discouraging the use of new materials, and by rejecting any futurist design.

The way that fashion has been thematized, indeed, contrasts with the saying that "sólo los crotos y los lingeras visten mal en Argentina." The way that fashion has been articulated still preserves an understanding of being in the pampas, an understanding that is manifest in its boundaries, and *in its claims with regard to truth.* What is put aside in the distinction between *tener* and *ser*, and what the default enables us to glimpse, is that *fashion displays truth*, the *ἄπειρον* character of truth.

For making manifest this displaying of truth we may focus our attention in the months before the murderous events of New Rome. The legion left Buenos Aires by ship, heading South, perhaps avoiding one of the paradoxes of the pampas. When they finally arrived at *Fuerte Argentino*, the troops landed wearing bright uniforms, suede boots, hats with feathers. Furthermore, the request of these lavish uniforms is one that appears at the top in the list of requests that Olivieri sent to former president Mitre (Article 1, Decree from November 22, 1855; Article 19th of the organization project for the Military Colony). Why so much display of design, why so much concern for the cut if one is to go to the South, to the middle of the pampas, to nowhere? Being takes place in the pampas, and fashion displays this taking place, or rather, what exceeds the display, the lavishness of being. *Prêt-à-porter* in the pampas means "ready to be exhibited," but also "ready to be gossiped about," "ready for the spreading," ready for the Heideggerian idle talk; and indeed, as something that appears as part of an ordinary world.

Fashion unconceals truth; it says "what you see with your eyes is also in being." Indeed, temporality persists on thematizing fashion in terms of "the cut": a new trend, an asymmetrical cut, ... Fashion confronts chronology, and not only because of its way of displaying its extension, its taking place, or the turmoils that it generates, but also because fashion appeals to regress *ad infinitum*, and to the idea of alteration as a positive phenomenon—for it fits our bodies, and compels us to be aware of our being flesh. Every season fashion proposes new forms and colors designed to provoke, to seduce, to inspire, to call into attention, to do what language calls into the question of its reality: shrug the shoulders and merely say, merely recall, the impossibility of being in the pampas as a *nostalgia del presente*. "En aquéiso momento el hombre se digo: / que no daría yo por la dicha / de estar a tu lado en Islandia / bajo el gran día inmóvil / y de compartir el ahora / como se comparte la música / o el sabor de una fruta / En aquel precise momento / el hombre estaba junto a ella en Islandia" (Borges, *Obras Completas*, III, 317).

Once lost in the cover, the demand for novelty compells us to hear and understand beforehand what is said in the talk of fashion.

One may notice, then, that being in the pampas is displayed in a cut, in certain discontinuity that unfolds into shapes that did not quite take place before. It is not only that fashion makes us aware of being in the pampas with one another, but also that in any chatty, loud mouthed retelling, one finds oneself immersed in the talk: wondering, astonished, overwhelmed by all that can take place in the pampas, challenging our fore-having of austerity and asceticism (Aira, *Ema, la Cautiva,* 94–97). Further, the "dictum" of fashion, the pronouncement with regard to the cut is not opposed to the genuineness of being, for it is not *ὅρος*. Fashion only requires giving credit to what one sees, and to unfold the possibility that one may also become a mimesis of the cut—wear *that,* look like *that.*

In this discourse, the relationship to being in the pampas can be appropriated in a primordial manner, but communicates rather by following the route of gossiping and passing the world along: *κόρος,* satiety, exigency, and indeed encouragement: what is said in the talk spreads in wider circles with fluidity, and takes on an authoritative character only possible because of its being groundless. The groundlessness of fashion, its taking place as *Dasein* unfolds truth about our own body: its apeiron character, by compelling our bodies to confront with images of what is in being, images that say something, anything with regard to our own image.

A different demand is also posited by fashion: philosophical discourses on being in the pampas must acknowledge the human body, and the way embodiment exceeds any distinction between *tener* and *ser.* This demand serves to keep our bodily being in the pampas open for us in an articulated, bodily understanding, rather than a display in the mere sense of "showing off." The aim of fashion is not that of deception, but that of unfolding what is in being. A man wearing a *bombín* which he does not take off even when sleeping or a man rigorously wearing a gray suit, glasses, and necktie Eton-style are to be scorned, humiliated, and compelled to adopt the manners of many. The turmoil, the revolt produced by the groundless taking place of fashion is proof against its shallow character. Uncontrollably, it gets passed along in further retelling, an act that is misunderstood by temporalizing ontology, for it amounts to perverting the act of disclosing being, what is underneath. Fashion, particularly futurist fashion, stands in the pampas, and exhibits something that is not yet interpreted by the exigency of blue jeans and a feminine Che Guevara t-shirt, or even the black leather jacket, and the gray suit, which are forms of fastening, bounding beings.

Futurist fashion, by its very nature, produces idle talk because it threatens the unchangeable and untranslatable nature of *ser*. It is always already making demands for more being, for excess, for *κόρος* on our very being in the pampas: highways, fast cars, mobile phones, electronics, magnetic trains, international style on our buildings, satellites ... cruelty itself, our becoming other already advanced in the poem *Martín Fierro*.

Borges narrates how "An old sword, a leather frame, containing the daguerreotype of a blank-faced man with a beard, the dash and grace of certain music, the familiar strophes of Martín Fierro, the passing years, boredom and solitude, all went to foster this voluntary, but never ostentatious nationalism ..." gives shape to Dalhman's southern destiny (Borges, *Ficciones*, 167). What Borges displays—and what fashion challenges—is how the dominance of the public way in which things have been interpreted has already been decisive even for events of a single life. In their "*bravuconadas*" as well as in their silence, the *they* prescribes one's wearings, thereby controlling any excess, ensuring that the South is always to be conceived temporally, as an "ancient and sterner world" (*Ficciones*, 169).

Fashion, which shows things off in the way we perceive the exuberance and lavishness of being, remains unsaid by two temporal prejudices: its inappropriateness for the pampas (its calling other beings into display), and its seasonal—cyclical, *mimetic*—character; both challenging the temporalizing way of thinking being: how is it possible for futurist fashion to take place, to be fully manifest in the pampas, isn't is *desubicado*, out of place? Why fashion is not persistent, present-at-hand, like a leather jacket? Isn't all this a concern for the very few? One *must* remain cut off, marginal, ascetic, to any display of forms that belong to the other world, a world that is defined in terms of "temporal" distances—as long as fashion takes place *in time*—and foreign, displaced, and indeed, recognizable when it comes to matters of territoriality, of vicinity. To adopt a futurist fashion (a pair of polyurethane pants, a Fendi watch, man-made shoes, a yellow beret, green eye shades), implies certain resoluteness, and certain involvement with clothes: a cyclical and proper character of being in the pampas. What is understood as merely having is an exhibition of being, of *truth:* what you see with your eyes is also in being, and it is calling to take place here too. This stubborn claim is its reality. Yet this reality demands to be invisible, a self-assurance beyond the boldness of average ways of looking and thinking of fashion.

As a phenomenon that takes place in the pampas, fashion displays truth as lavishness, excess, *ἄπειρον.* It calls to our attention the dualfold nature of the inquiry we pursue: its inner ambiguity, its suggestion that a description of events may take place, does not preclude giving in advance a view about the way the history of ontology has been thematized. We have made explicit that in any temporalizing account of history of ontology, being must always be related to *time* in such a way that our concerns may fall into chronology and into the form of doxography. We have also made explicit that such an account of the history of ontology arbitrarily ignores the question of *place,* for *place* itself has been thematized as a phenomenon dependent on time, irrelevant in and of itself for the most part. Under time, *place* becomes an anecdote, a certain rumor that is completely marginal to philosophy, ancillary, and for the most part full of local colors, as opposed to the universalism claimed by temporality. Time has, in turn, also been split into "divisible" spans, and has brought up the discussion of the discontinuity of the territory as the discussion of "nation."

Fashion, with its many tendencies, displays ways of being in the middle of the pampas that may be hidden, or rather, remain unsuspected, unveiled. It displays a tendency towards seeing, it demands to be seen. Heidegger called such a tendency *curiosity,* for it is not merely confined to seeing, but as a tendency towards a peculiar way of letting the world be encountered by us in perception, one that exceeds cognition, a tendency already manifest in Greek thinkers who conceived of cognition in terms of *desire to see.* Is curiosity a preliminary step toward *μίμησις*? What is the relation between curiosity and the taking place of being in fashion? Parmenides' poem already related the perceptive understanding of being with displaying: a goddess without name pointing at images on a cave wall. A goddess who is taking care that the young Parmenides will not take the path of non-being, as if what the images display were not present in being.

Thus, curiosity detaches itself from the way of thematizing the history of ontology offered by temporality, for it focuses on the rumor, on the spreading, on the scandal of any new design, and its taking place here and there; and scandal within which one may came to forget where one is, its *"justo lugar,"* one's being in the pampas immersed in default. Both in fashion and in ontology, "there is no novelty without risk"; futurist fashion may appear too risky, too shallow, or too astounding to be taken seriously, but it is also too apeiron to be anticipated or even rejected.

Philosophers, at most, can observe the remarkable priority of seeing, and repeat Augustine's remarks in connection with *concupiscentia. "Ad oculus enim videre proprie pertinet* (Seeing belongs properly to the eyes) (quoted in Heidegger, *Being and Time*, 215). But, doesn't fashion overturn this sense of *cognoscendum*, the very *'neque enim dicimus: aidi quir rutilet; aut, olfac wuam niteat; aut, gusta quam splendeat; aut, palpa quam fulgeat; videre enim dicitur haec omnia'* (For we do not say 'hear how it glows,' or 'smell how it glistens,' or 'taste how is shines,' or 'feel how it flashes,' but we say of each 'see'; we say that all this is seen')?" Isn't the lust of the eye something yet to take place in the pampas?

Curiosity, then, enables us to glimpse possibilities that may be part of a betrayal, and a reversal, the very being other. Borges, whose concerns never excluded fashion, made manifest that this may be the case in the pampas. His counterposing the warrior and the captive is a way of displaying that excess, that cruelty of being other. Droctulft was suddenly "blinded and renewed by the City, that revelation" (Borges, *Collected Fictions*, 209). Then, the cruelty, the extension of himself beyond himself: "He knows that in this city he will be a dog, or a child, and that he will not even begin to understand it, but he knows as well that this city is worth more than his gods and the faith he is sworn to and all the marshlands of Germany. Droctulft deserts his own kind and fights for Ravenna" (*Collected Fictions*, 209). Equally, the captive is also subject to *ἄπειρον*: "One day my grandmother, half in wonder, half in jest, remarked upon her fate—an Englishwoman torn from her country and her people and carried to this far end of the earth. The person to whom she made the remark told her she wasn't the only one, and months later pointed out to an Indian girl slowly crossing the town square. She was barefoot, and wearing two red ponchos; the roots of her hair were blond," the fairness of her complexion is doubled by "her coppery face painted with fierce colors, her eyes were that half-hearted blue that the English call gray" (*Collected Fictions*, 210).

An Englishwoman, coming from the pampas, from the hinterland, talking to another Englishwoman who is to go through cruelty. Then the defiance, the reluctance to go back to *civilization*. In her eyes "one caught glimpses of a savage and uncouth life: tents of horsehide, fires fueled by dung, celebrations in which the people feasted on meat singed over the fire or on raw viscera, stealthy marches at dawn; the raid on the corrals, the alarm sounded, the plunder, the battle, the thundering round up of the starkly naked horsemen, polygamy, stench, and magic" (*Collected Fictions*, 210). Then, Borges unfolds the reluctance to admit this doubling of the bodies: "An English woman reduced to such a barbarism!" (*Collected Fictions*, 210), and the scandal of the impossible "the other woman answered that she has happy, and she returned that night to the desert" (*Collected Fictions*, 210–211); she "leaped to the ground and drank up the hot blood" (*Collected Fictions*, 211). If such a betrayal, such a reversal is to be accomplished, we are compelled toward cruelty: it is not enough to embrace the cycles, to look for uncertainty, it is an exigency to adopt the most extravagant and provocative fashion (futurist, minimalist, with man-made materials, plastic bags) in order to make explicit being in the pampas as *ἄπειρον*.

Those who deny in advance this possibility show contempt for the circularity of this thinking: if idle talk, retelling, controls the ways in which one may be curious, and fashion is thematized by curiosity, then how can fashion exercise influence over idle talk? Besides, why should we adopt Japanese designs in the pampas? What is the meaning of such an attempt? When we talk about the risk of fashion we have already implied that fashion goes beyond the fore-having and the fore-conceptions posited in both idle talk and curiosity. This phenomenon is manifest in the becoming other, in the radical mimesis, the assertiveness that fashion offers. Curiosity, for which nothing is closed off, holds fast to fashion and evinces the possibility of taking place in one's own body. Idle talk, for which there is nothing that is not understood, provides enough justifications, encouragement, to acquire and to become other, an inclination toward lavishness that breaks off the circle imposed by the distinction between *tener* and *ser*. But this can be better understood by means of display.

The present exposition with regard to fashion can be also clarified by means of the Eleatic paradoxes, for fashion also demands to be thought as *ἄπειρον*, as taking place and exceeding its place, as something that one can not get through step by step; and as something unlimited. One may say, for instance, that a pair of polyester pants call for a striped rayon shirt, a pair of blue square glasses matching with blue shoes. Is this fashion to take place in the pampas? Further, why is it that the slowest change in fashion, a new cut, can never be overtaken by the swiftest buyers? Isn't this already a perpetual race like that of Achilles? Are we then to conclude that fashion cannot take place in the pampas, arguing that a buyer must always buy half of the designs in order to be fashionable, and even before half of the half, and half of the half of the half, and before half of the half of the half of the half.... Aren't the distances growing? Or, finally, are we going to claim that each item of cloth encloses *ἄπειρον* designs?

Temporality seems to resist the conclusion we have been drawing all along with regard to images, signs, and now with regard to fashion. Eleatic philosophers pointed out that the only way to overcome paradox is by means of exceeding its place, by means of extension, of cruelty. We can trace this taking place in Argentinean literature, from Estanislao del Campo's gaucho in a theatre house, to Carriego, that "consumptive youth, dressed in black, who used to saunter among the single-story houses of Palermo, trying out a line or stopping now and again to look at something he was soon to leave behind" (Borges, *Evaristo Carriego,* 164).

Curiosity, as a mean of excess, does not let us remain undecided, putting some distance between what is already there and oneself. When looking at someone's futurist style or appearance one is confronted with what Heidegger called "resoluteness": the other is proximally there, exceeding anything that *they* have heard about—say in their talk—and what they know about his or her clothes. We have described this phenomenon as "censorship," the addition of details ... something that Aira thematized in *Ema, la Cautiva* with regard to mintage: the lavishness of being, reality given itself completely, a *patacón,* "the treasure of the poor" (Aira, *Ema, la Cautiva,* 95). But fashion is a phenomenon that may not be fully displayed until we exceed our thematizing of being in purely temporal terms and we give a different, *ἄπειρον,* meaning to our displayings—beyond ascetism, beyond boredom, beyond solitude.

Like fashion, like image, like any sign, "the hare," and "the duck's egg" are involved in a continuum of retellings, of gossip that frees to circulation what temporal ontology intends to remain "a fixed language that posterity would have to accept for what it is would be like a hen hatching a duck's egg: the language: the language created by him would be borne along, willy-nilly, by the current that engulfs all language." (*Course in General Linguistics*, 151). In such a politics of hocus-pocus there is always the risk of displacing the sign. But this phenomenon will not be explicit until the excess of signs offers itself in a sort of continuum with mintage, for the duck's egg can be paralleled to convertibility. The task of ontology in the pampas is to exhibit this way of taking place in which signs always "exceed that which is indicated."

Such an interpretation of signs should not merely provide support for a characterization of reference. It must exhibit how alteration takes place in signs, to the point that signs shift from being ready to hand as a certain tool to become a tool in the default, the other of any tool. The way signs call for other signs: the way the leather pants call for the rayon shirt, the rayon shirt calls for the glasses, and so on.

The Libertador

Every day, after I taught my class, I strode to the radio station. To listen to a live show playing those records that now I miss. To recognize the voice of the woman who announced the exchange rate every morning. A woman who gaped, full of delight, when someone mocked her hair. She is also a body.

Behind her, the Libertador did not move, except by shrinking his shoulders twice. He was still looking aside, for he always managed to look toward the East. To the many seats that are in her office, the many seats that were empty that day. A general, a storyteller. For many, a nihilist. The biggest ever born in South America. For some, a drunk man and a violent husband. But these things made him only human. He belonged to the land insofar as he knew how to resign. And for him, that effort was minimal.

We got along perhaps because we had very little, almost nothing in common. Now I realize that in the pampas people don't really talk. They manage to interpose many circumstances between them. If they do, it is only to find out that they are poles apart. She showed nothing but contempt for my hair, my stories, or the fact that I am so young. Days before that meeting, she took the opinion that I did not really deserve my luck, whatever it might bring. So she assigned me unbearable tasks. And she picked on my attitude several times. On my making excuses not to lower the flag. She did not understand that the flag was just right where it was, for it cast shade. She might have been cruel, but she was not. I am unable to tell why she talked like the loving mother we never needed.

It was in her office where she asked him, in the most impersonal way—that is, using "tenés que"—to organize the school festival for the Libertador's day, in August. He might not have gone then, and that is precisely why she was thinking about him. For, one needs to think about the future as if it were present.

Once I cited passages from Pausanias and Plato in order to clarify a remark, but I was not understood. Some other time I showed a vase with Greek figures to the students to explain the meaning of the poem. I do not know if these recollections are now part of someone else's anecdote.

Mintage

The former considerations make explicit that alteration and depreciation have to be thought in terms of *place.* Assertions such as "being is depreciated" or "being is hyperinflated" seem to point out the phenomenon of mintage as one that also always exceeds its place, and indeed one that lets us deduce the excess of being. In this sense, there is a reversal, a sense of inadequacy in thinking the political problem of the discontinuity of the territory in terms of overproduction and underconsumption. We have attempted to interpret Olivieri's intentions as denouncing underproduction in the pampas as a need for excess that is not explicit until one sees images.

Arguably, this interpretation runs against that of traditional ontology, for it demands that we persistently focus our attention on the retellings, gossipings that provide stories that increase the misunderstandings in the rather whimsical desire to give reports. Circulation moves within a flux beyond chronology. This flux—or rather, the excess of flux—is presupposed in mintage conceived as a way of solving the discontinuity of the territory: it ensures that mintage is to exceed the territory itself. Our philosophical task then is to display how this continuum takes place and to inquire if this phenomenon has to do with the goddess's suggestion of not cutting off what is in being from holding fast to what is in being.

We are familiar with the fact that what is in being is subject to the alteration, depreciation, and overvaluation of a certain situation, for this is a phenomenon that we grasp in our everydayness. We are also acquainted with the philosophical anthropology that some have derived from this phenomenon, but we have shown that this is a task that only competes with historical ontology. Contrary to the spirit of our time of turmoil, we are to focus our attention on the excess brought by monetary policies: mintage, depreciation; but also alteration itself—the alteration of clothes, the alteration of images, the alteration of signs, the alteration of coins—for these unveil a circumspective concern on "*no dañar la image,*" on "giving a good impression" (Cf. Aira, *Ema, la Cautiva*, 185–189).

Besides, mintage itself reveals the captiveness of the captive. This is to be understood in two senses that must exceed themselves: (i) in the sense that captivity is a condition for mintage; and (ii) in the sense that the captive exhibits the conditions manifest in mintage, both in terms of body and in terms of couture. To a certain extent, the captive fully displays in herself the economy of alteration: the fact that a body admits changes—as if the body takes more or less place than it actually takes—within the same kind from a lesser to a greater or from a greater to a lesser; but in any case addressing the exigency: that of looking nice, of "giving a good impression" (Cf. Aira, *Ema, la Cautiva*, 185–189).

Alteration is dogmatically believed to be a phenomenon that takes place in time. This is the way that temporality has conceived ontology, as temporal being, even though it may acknowledge as a *possibility* being defined in terms of lesser and greater. Accordingly, alteration is a change in the exchange value of things that happens at certain *nows* that may have something to do with *other* nows. This phenomenon, this increase or decrease in value, is registered on exchange rate currency boards. But this *in* seems to imply that alteration takes place by taking more than its place, by exceeding its place. This is manifested in the concern for a good impression, not in the value displayed by the currency itself.

Indeed, this phenomenon is exhibited differently by convertibility. Convertibility has grounded itself on this simple truism: a law may place value beyond any rumor, restraining, bounding what is to be said. Convertibility of currency ensures its place as long as those bills, whose value exchanges are faithfully used in payments, are "available," or rather "present-at-hand" for the State in case it can not fulfill the payment of debt. The nature of law keeps one silent on the exchange rate, on this unusual transformation from a piece of colored paper into a dollar. "In matters like these, it's important to win people's belief. But in this particular case, it so happens that we Mapuche have no need to believe in anything, because we've always known that changes of this kind occur" (Aira, *The Hare,* 26). Indeed, for this change to take place, it demands a certain captivity, a certain *ajuste,* and "whitening." Furthermore, it cannot evolve without a notion of territoriality as exceeding the territory. It is necessary to display that fact in the captive itself, for the captive is the very symbol of a continuum grounded on cruelty: that of the captivity of savings.

With the default, and the return to more traditional ways of mintage, the captive still keeps her basic notes. Indeed, captivity is, first and foremost, that of the rumor. Power is not enough, not even relevant in this circumstance. Aira has depicted this phenomenon in Carhué. What we need to see is that these rumors are not like any other rumor. Espina ensures us that "the most alarming rumors circulated about him" (*Ema, la Cautiva,* 24). But these rumors are to be exceeded: if they "painted him as a semi-savage, with indian blood in his veins, enthused by terror, and tyrannical in the highest degree" (*Ema, la Cautiva,* 24), they let us see that "at the dinner attended, besides the commander and Lieutenant Lavalle, two other officers, the conversation unfolded in French from the beginning to the end" (*Ema, la Cautiva,* 24).

Within mintage, then, we are all involved in a double game of impression. Men appear "unfamiliar. You must have seen them: painted, wearing feathers ... a big spectacle. It seems that they came from far away" (*Ema, la Cautiva,* 27). Mintage finds its justification in a survival that takes place today, by passing over in silence any regard for the money borrowed to pay for that luxury, the bureaucracy of being. To a certain extent one is to indulge, for "in any case, everything is forgiven to them in the name of their miraculous aptitude to survive, even though the use that this survival may have for us is more than disputable" (*Ema, la Cautiva,* 29).

There are some who point to the fact that once one embraces a new coinage, one is compelled to become otherwise. To say it differently, one is better identified by one's "belongingness" that has taken place *in advance:* one "belongs to that cast of opulent barbarians, eloquent in transformations of fortune, who are always full, even though they are magnets for misery" (*Ema, la Cautiva,* 29). Circulation itself moves around, disperses, holds fast and never cut off, but does it exceed itself? Are there restrictions with regard to the phenomenon of "whitening" and the questions of territoriality? When Aira asks, "But, isn't trade with Indians forbidden?" (*Ema, la Cautiva,* 30), he has already acknowledged that convertibility demands a "whitening" of funds as a necessary step toward the taxability of being. Its major cruelty, its way of doubling the bodies is, indeed, to push them toward the margins, toward non-being, for

> the law does not have such a long arm. Everything done from here on—he made an imaginary line in space with a sweeping gesture toward the West—responds to no legislation. But look how curious it is: I do not think that with his traffic Espina is violating any order, for he does so with the money he himself launched, so that for the central government that business positively does not exist. (*Ema, la Cautiva,* 30)

This carrying away, this motion toward the South (the "ancient and stern" South) that goes beyond the simple "whitening"—which seems to be rather paradoxical as the many stories of the captive display—is to be thought in terms of desertion, for "beyond a certain limit (and as we continue together through the pampas you need to get used to the fact that here we are always talking about limits and borders) everything is desertion, for no one is in one's proper place" (*Ema, la Cautiva,* 31).

Once placed in the margins, it is natural to think in terms of *ἄπειρον*, in terms of excess that one can not get through. Ontologically, the question of being in the pampas is manifest as a question of place. As for mintage, the archetype of women, the captive, also becomes the archetype of circulation, for the captive exhibits two properties: that of endless reproducibility and that of *ἄπειρον* exchangeability. The first one is, perhaps, a tribute to liberal policies: "Women do nothing but procreate.... If they are not impregnated by their husbands, they are impregnated by the soldiers who go and visit them all the time. The flux of births is constant, continuous, unlimited, and it remains in suspense, without denouement.... Isn't it odd? So far no one has figured out how to take advantage of this situation" (*Ema, la Cautiva,* 35).

As for their exchangeability, the use of captives as currency, Espina turns it into a futile spectacle compared to his bills—both as a spectacle that took place before and is to take place again, and one that is rather useless: "the famous exchange of women is a commonplace in ethnology. When you see it with your own eyes, you will find that it is innocuous, innocent theater, and rather useless, like everything else" (*Ema, la Cautiva,* 47). Within the pampas, the fortune of men is not better. To a certain extent, they also have been embraced by captivity. A soldier placed at the frontier is first and foremost (i) "a forced draftee, like everyone else, who spent more than ten years at the border" (ii) "(someone who) had gone through all the vicissitudes of melancholy"; (iii) "Of affable character, kind, and courteous almost to the point of exaggeration"; (iv) "Passionate about gambling or fishing"; (v) "Although he is probably not forty yet, his ascetic and emaciated face has deep wrinkles and gray hair"; (iv) "Some time ago he was promoted to corporal, and then demoted because of something he had done. None of which bothered him in the least" (*Ema, la Cautiva,* 77).

If mintage ensures a perpetual display of fashion at the frontier, this onerous spreading of rumors and scandals, this infinite dispersion of the event into other events always manifests a regress *ad infinitum*—as long as satiety produces insolence, and indeed, satiety depends on a certain temporal stillness: the moment of introducing coinage. That is the moment of expectation that precedes, or rather, produces the rumors that ensure the value of the bills.

> The conversation had reached an impasse. The men were silent, and the horses shifted restlessly in their place. Finally, the colonel gave an order to the lieutenant, who returned to the fortress at full gallop. Less than five minutes after (everything was already set up), he left the fortress, this time very slowly, in the middle of a silence in which one could hear the crickets. Behind him, came a voluminous cart pulled by two oxen. The load was covered by a canvas, and it wobbled as if it were about to tip. All the spectators

> were convinced that this was a show. That the load must be a sort of ransom in exchange for which the Indians would suspend the imaginary *malón*. When they were to cross the stream, they asked some curious onlookers for help who somehow managed to peek at the load and who had spread the rumor: that the load was money, paper bills, and packaged wads. Many refused to believe it, for if that were the case, the quantity of bills must be colossal. (*Ema, la Cautiva*, 87)

By spreading rumors, mintage postpones the *malón*, and ensures the emergence of a government grounded on mintage. Indeed, mintage is grounded on certain premises: (i) Circulation must take place; (ii) The territory is *apeiron;* (iii) Circulation is given in advance, and in this sense, it is the ground for the continuum; (iv) Censorship must be abolished, and/or centralized; (v) Circulation demands recovery of the laughter afterwards (indeed, "one is no worse than before"). Aira narrates "an Indian lifted a corner of the canvas, and he stirred the bills with the tip of his spear. Without saying another word, he moved to the coachman's seat, and he slowly drove away" (*Ema, la Cautiva*, 87).

This series of rumors, misapprehensions, misunderstandings, endless retellings taking place around the continuum of currency, displaces cruelty and delays it by making historicality manifest. "I think the colonel has found the simplest system of avoiding wars—said one of the witnesses with irony. I don't know why this didn't occur to anyone earlier!" (*Ema, la Cautiva*, 88). The history of ontology, then, becomes the other of a story, a reversal, a motion inside out that ensures the emergence of a hyperinflated government by means of mintage. Yet, this excessive form of government ensures its own historicizing. "Stripped of its foliage, history is no more than a succession of payments, the more exorbitant, the better. The only thing that has changed has been the form and the credit" (*Ema, la Cautiva*, 88). Furthermore, it demands that a certain territory must be exceeded, a territory given in advance: Currency must gain a place, take place before men inhabit such a territory.

It was after the embarrassment of the Falklands' war that we came to realize this way of conceiving territoriality in terms of mintage given in advance: Argentineans never wanted to move to—needless to say live in—these gelid islands; they just wanted to ensure that our bills were there, standing in reserve. In this sense it is to be understood that "war has never taken place. The proof of this is that it could always be suspended" (*Ema, la Cautiva,* 88). The same may hold for the expression *"volveremos."*

Besides revealing this notion of territoriality, mintage needs to exhibit, to make fully visible for further retellings its arbitrariness if it wants to ensure the other of any form of despotism (Cf. Aira, *Ema, la Cautiva,* 151–168). One retelling: "Mintage is an arbitrary construction, an element chosen only because of its utility to pass the time. Those bills were minted by the colonel. It is enough for him to put in use, every time he wants, the minting machine that the Frenchman built for him" (*Ema, la Cautiva,* 88). What keeps people on the edge of their ontological chair, then, is the possibility of launching new coins or bills; temporally; what matters is *the next bill* (even though one may still find that in certain places people use the bills launched by Urquiza). These three notes imply a change in the focus, from the circulation itself, and its fashionable impression, to an inquiry concerning the temporal origin of money: the mintage machine, the arbitrary decision of a colonel. Once this arbitrariness is manifested as involuntary, unconscious, there is only one necessary step to free circulation and the fashionable design of bills. Aira's solution to the political problem of the Huiliche—that of the discontinuity of the territory—has been solved by means of a reduction in the powers of the state, a sort of last resource: the return to a minimal state, a hyperinflated state that grants the right of mintage to any individual, in a way that the responsibility of the individual also becomes infinite, unlimited, boundless, like taxes. Fashion, then, already frees itself from accusations of "puerility." The frivolous itself is used "to unleash the circulation of money, which in any other way would be troublesome to distribute" (*Ema, la Cautiva,* 88).

Historically, mintage always "sets a precedent. From now on, perhaps every war may be just that, a comedy of extortion and ransom payments. A new genre. It can put in motion the tribes of the external circuit, and invests tons of bills every week" (*Ema, la Cautiva,* 89). Indeed, mintage must also face the problem of social justice that it claims to solve in advance, for the money put into circulation may only go "into the hands of one or two *caciques,* or perhaps to Cafúl hands only" (*Ema, la Cautiva,* 89). To bring circulation into perfection, distribution must take place with excess, beyond expectations. Mintage relies on such an assumption. "To Cafúl, or to whomever, that money will be useless unless he succeeds in distributing it. At least, to distribute enough bills to create an 'environment' of money" (89). Temporality, then, is forced to bring back the problem of the destiny of money, for nothing ensures that the chieftains may spend the money between them, "in political payments" (*Ema, la Cautiva*, 89). This is, in the end, a risk that an emergent government grounded on circulation as such is compelled to take, perhaps under the assumption that "sooner or later, money always filters from the rich to the poor" (89) whether by means of political payments or by gambling. Politically, "gambling is no more than a lubricant of circulation. One may say that it is circulation itself, in its fastest aspect" (*Ema, la Cautiva*, 89), yet "circulation is based on continuity—someone else advanced—while the changes of fortune in gambling are interrupted by nature" (*Ema, la Cautiva*, 89), moreover, "In gambling—said another—one always loses everything, so that there is concentration, but a negative one. It can not be a good method of dispensing goods" (*Ema, la Cautiva*, 90).

The *μίμησις* in circulation is both restricted, for it consists in the initial mintage—and unbounded—*ἄπειρον*, for once in circulation, any bill will exceed itself, its nominal value. That is the reason why circulation is not essentially temporal: "Espina is not God, and it is not so idiotic to imitate Him beyond mere formalities. He began by creating money. Now it would be the moment to create the thing upon which to use it. But Espina withdraws himself. This second step does not concern him. He only wants to make circulation perfect" (*Ema, la Cautiva*, 90). Circulation exceeds itself regardless of time.

Mintage itself, as a monetary solution, demands reconsideration of the question of place, for if the circulation of coins and bills exceeds their place, place must necessarily exist, not only as a territory exceeding its boundaries, but also as a void. "In the same way that a void can attract to it everything that is within its reach, Espina thought, a space that is too full could expel, toward a certain person, all the value or value itself" (*Ema, la Cautiva*, 93). Espina's reasonings echo the Eleatic thinkers and Pindar with regard to *κόρος*, for "how could any one fill the world with excess? What is 'full,' by definition, is never 'full enough'" (*Ema, la Cautiva*, 93). To the problem of the void, "Espina's answer was money, and its quantities. In fact, nothing can be filled with excess, but only when it is about definite objects. Excess is an *ἐπιφαινόμενον* of money, and it is doubtful that it could be excess without immense and incommensurable quantities of money" (*Ema, la Cautiva,* 93). Political economy in the pampas is to be thought of in terms of this monetary excess as an aesthetic phenomenon that displays being and its cruelty.

Naturally, once mintage took place, as suddenly as it began, the excess was followed by monstrous cycles of depreciation, circulation and betrayal.* That is its cruelty, its doubling the bodies. "The village was flooded with bills. The salary of the soldiers was increased a hundredfold. Espina backed his printing press with his collection of Indian money; the Indians put their bills beyond any backing, in the absolute" (*Ema, la Cautiva,* 94). This scandalous delight in the impossible, this placing of truth, this exaggerated celebration implies that limits are not vessels, but boundless, porous, images, in such a way that it is not impossible to deliver them to England.

> Is it true that the colonel shipped millions and millions of the new bills to England? It is not impossible. If his idea was from the very beginning to think of the savage kingdom as a territory without limits (for not even savagery itself, as his manners well proved, was a limit), an archipelago as distant as Great Britain may also partake of it. For the moment, he ordered a portrait of her Majesty next to his own in pounds. (*Ema, la Cautiva,* 94)

Very few now remember that convertibility brought the luxury inherent in any human act—the cruelty of satiety, the lavishness, the fattiness of being. "Although common people could barely see them pass by, and enter the fortress, they could not resist admiring the richness and magnificence of these courts" (*Ema, la Cautiva,* 95).

Mintage, in its initial stage, challenged the assumptions of those who adopt the ascetism of being as a principle and who reason from the distinction between *tener* and *ser.* They found themselves mistaken, "They had thought that frivolity had no more secrets for them, but now they realized that they were mistaken. What they were witnessing was not even dreamt by them" (*Ema, la Cautiva,* 96). If the bills "of the colonel had reached their remote addressee, and now answers started coming back, answers that—being about money—could not be less than luxurious answers and infinite possibilities, the complete reality, the treasure of the poor" (*Ema, la Cautiva,* 95), what are we to be afraid of, then? What is so embarrassing in this excess? Is it really going to distract us from the discontinuity of the territory, or manifest the continuum? What else is to be enjoyed in the name of *ser* if being is *ἄπειρον*? What is in being is to be manifested in the numerous crowds, their inner dissemination of a philosophy of excess yet to take place. Aira relates how

> lately, the embassies became more numerous. The entourages opted not to enter the fortress, instead they waited for their lords in the meadows around the stream, in the forest shade. The whole hamlet and the tamed Indians attended; and the contact with the foreigners lasted for days. People drank and smoked in lapses of pure magic. Those were days of learning, of looking and imitating. At the beginning, they thought of everything they saw as so cunning that they did not feel confident enough to imitate it. But novelty overpowered them like an irresistible wave. (*Ema, la Cautiva,* 95)

Novelty, *μίμησις* itself, manifests itself in an exuberance that is still unknown but is suspected, for "Very frequently, two or more retinues coming from different places converged. In those cases, a whole tournament of elegance took place in front of the villagers' almost incredulous gaze. It was not until then that they understood how much they pondered interior life; for the Indians could give them lessons on asceticism: that which was not appearance was disparaged" (*Ema, la Cautiva,* 96). They came to understand that being in the pampas was justified as an aesthetic phenomenon "standing in reserve." And yet, all this motion was grounded on stillness, that of mintage.

Circulation compelled people to become cruel, to take the risk the continuum imposes upon itself, to acknowledge the possibility that being in the pampas can only be justified as a lavish aesthetic phenomenon, Men of solid figure appeared "painted from head to toes"; moreover, "they plucked their eyebrows and eyelashes. They wore golden bracelets, thick and flexible, to concentrate energy. They tied their arms and legs with cotton bands. On their fingers, they wore dozens of rings. They used to take them off, as if they were gloves, to throw the dice with particular effectiveness" (*Ema, la Cautiva,* 96). But all this was only real, cruelty itself after the default.

Cruelty is to be thought as a multiplication, a proliferation of gestures, contortions, extravagant movements, colors, suffering and greed that had already taken possession of us, and turned us finally to exhibit the fashionable painting of bodies:

> defying any explanation, they were out of painting itself. Centuries ago, they started to give a great aesthetic value to messiness. Now they imitate the causal fluttering of a butterfly with their powders

> or with the trickle of a sponge soaked up in black ink pressed against their chests; a flickering squared design on a Hercules; a warrior with blue spotted arms, completely covered with fast brush strokes that crack once dried. (*Ema, la Cautiva*, 97)

In any case, being exceeds its forms, its images, its clothes, its suggestions in ways that are denied to take place in the pampas because we refuse to admit that being is excessive, that being exceeds mintage itself: "Many of them wear a shaved and mottled head; silvered skulls were in fashion. Most of them showed off horse-like hair styles impregnated with rare oils" (*Ema, la Cautiva*, 97).

If among the Eleatic philosophers, Empedocles of Acagras could claim that "love was the beginning of everything," Espina improved this gracious expression: with circulation and exchange, these forms of alteration, "everything was sexuality and love. According to Espina, love began with banking" (*Ema, la Cautiva*, 98). With the bank, captivity exceeds itself.

Ema herself exhibits this excess from the beginning. "Why is it the case that pregnant women take so much space. I cannot ponder the reason ... it is beyond my comprehension. It is as if they themselves become space" (*Ema, la Cautiva*, 117). Captivity, then, takes place as reproducibility, as "more children for the fatherland." Yet, are these children given in advance? Do they ensure captivity? Reproducibility in time has turned women into the other of mintage, into a mirror of mintage. "It is true" says Ema, "there is no woman in the village who is not pregnant. What else can they do? They spend their time, at least. Besides, that is why they are sent to the dessert, to populate it" (*Ema, la Cautiva*, 117). The paradox is that if women take more space, and become more space, the space can never be filled, or with enough excess to.... Indeed, excess makes them aware of their finitude, of their condition of bounded-boundlessness, that "one can not get through." The impossible, devaluation itself, the manifestation of the other as other do not lead to the extinction of the Huiliche, but to their proliferation, to their excess in numbers and forms, without fashion and its manifestation in the pampas, for "in any other place we could all perish. But here, here death is impossible ... totally impossible. An absolute shelter" (*Ema, la Cautiva*, 118).

The cycles of depreciation manifest this taking place of being in the pampas, perhaps as an incongruence of being, as reality exceeding its boundlessness. "Reality, the perfect incongruence, must reach humanity at certain point" (*Ema, la Cautiva,* 169). The reality of the State is proved by its default, in the same way that the reality of the individual may be proved by "whitening" or "captivity." Being, the perfect incongruence, the disperser, the other becoming itself, the fashionable uptown cloth and veil, only points out, exhibits that what lies beneath is the State: "what is real, the minister told her, is the State. Its supreme proof consists in delegating in the individuals its only role, the mintage of currency" (*Ema, la Cautiva,* 169).

Why is this notion of the State as minimal so persistent in Argentinean literature, from the *Martin Fierro* to *The Hare,* and from the *Bases* to *Our poor individualism*? Did it take place in the pampas at all? As an excess? Are these lavish, frivolous multiplications running against a certain philosophical anthropology that bounds Argentines to be what they already are? What does it mean for Espina to launch bills *ad infinitum*? In *Ema, la Cautiva* we observe how money finds its justification as an aesthetic phenomenon, as an exhibition, as a garrulous promotion of the other that can take us out of boredom as nothing but a promise and not a program. Aira observes how

> everyone printed bills, and no one lacked means for doing so. It has always been like this, they maintained, from prehistory. But prehistory was another simulacrum. After all, the economy was the foundation of the only certainty that the Indians had: the impossibility of life. "Life is impossible" was the thought in its clearest and most definitive form, that is to say, a model that they always have in mind throughout their whole life. When procreating, staring at a passing by cloud, eating a quail's wing, swimming, waiting for their sleep to come . . . that was the only thing they knew; they did not count on anything else. (*Ema, la Cautiva,* 170)

What is impossible is always displayed in its possibilities; the impossible also manifests a certain tendency to exceed itself in such a way that it shows itself taking place in the most trifling events.

The function of currency may remain poorly understood within the boundaries of traditional ontology, which thematizes it only in terms of credit, exchange, and deferral instead of pointing out and showing that currency is a phenomenon that takes place and exceeds its place, in dispersion, in diffusion, in *ἄπειρον* exchanges. There is always a concern in admitting that currency takes place in such a way that it always multiplies the impossible, the incongruence, and—as fashion also does—points out its uncontrollable character, that once in circulation, it offers itself as a continuum that cannot be cut off. We did not enjoy enough of these bills, and we do not know all places that they can take. Aira, at least, notices that

> With their bills, they paid, they unceasingly paid; and they did not bother to do it, or perhaps, they were not quite aware of it. Drawers, sketchers, copyists, calligraphers . . . fantasy dictated to them the numbers and the premonition of death. Melancholy as an indifferent sphinx, uttered the numbers, indefinite ciphers, which turned voluminous in the sky. Life was still impossible, the prehistoric aesthetic ran away as much as their education. Their children learned how to use the minting machines before learning how to smoke, the eldest rested their heads on a roll soaked in ink to exhale their last breath. Even then, mintage was an activity whose secret remained ungraspable. "there is too much money," they said, "and life is too short." (*Ema, la Cautiva,* 170)

Unsuspected consequences, the politics of the unreal, the other of what is already known, took place: "Espina decided to take that step [to give a piece of land to those who asked for it] only when he ensured the financial conditions within which work could be absolutely unthinkable" (*Ema, la Cautiva,* 173).

The captive herself, as the prototype of such a dispersion, always embracing the cycles, turning away, leaving and loving, unveils other possibilities that circulation and time had ignored: production, *ποίησις*, ambition, the ever lasting peace.* Credit, then, is to be thought of as a spatial phenomenon. The greatest difficulty in understanding Huiliche political economy lies—as it is well known—in the fact that we enjoy "while in debt," and it is under this assumption that we take more credit, for debts do not have a correlation to time, to interest rates that in any case are *ἄπειρον*, but with the event of the *entrega*, the mintage, the circulation, the occasional fluidity, in such a way that "the terms of the credit could not be more liberal: an interest rate of one percent every five years, and a repayment due in four centuries. By then—he said laughing as if he were making a fantastic joke—none of us will be alive!" (*Ema, la Cautiva,* 175). The fact that a bill always exceeds its nominal value, and should be judged first and foremost by its prints—for aesthetics is secondary—is then exposed, fully displayed.

It is mistaken and misleading to think that its value is shown not in a *deferral* within a *promise* that is never fulfilled, but in dispersions, confusions, rumors, in the very fact that currency takes place. Currency itself makes fully manifest its value as *ποίησις*. "Some of them have brought infinite money—said the Indian woman. Do you see that one, seated next to my husband? He is the son of Mariano. He brought coins from the twilight bundled up in turtle and tiger paper cooked in the marshes" (*Ema, la Cautiva,* 195). Boundless notions of currency, in such a way that the exchange depends only on coming to be, in displaying what is also in being.

Mintage, the possibility of minting coins every time one needs them, suppresses the scandal—to admit that these bills do not exceed themselves into *ποίησις,* that they are kept as long as one borrows money to supplement or openly pay the salaries of government workers, for instance. Within temporality, mintage is delimited by its absurdity and greed. As in any financial talk,

> I have never spent an afternoon with so many alternatives. I cannot say that it was an absurd afternoon, at least not entirely. The lack of sense was always close to unleashing itself, but in the most crucial moment nothing really happened. Or better, there wasn't any crucial moment. Everything was repetition, what is called, precisely, an "enchanted afternoon." In those moments, one might think that an imminent scandal would stagger the sky. But the Indians do not know the scandal. Because it is human, it is human par excellence. (*Ema, la Cautiva,* 203)

Suddenly, our creditors were satiated by our infinite credits and our *ἄπειρον* excuses (*el rescate de la Cautiva, las nueve monedas de hierro, la calor*). Humanity, then, unfolded itself as inhuman, in a game of impressions, a sort of glimpse, "coinage is just an omnipotent instrument. Here, instead, it shows itself in its divine usefulness. I shuddered when I saw the rolls. It was evident that this wonderful veil (money), which hides everything, was drawn back. The masks are amulets. They may be used to suture the wholes produced by the transactions" (*Ema, la Cautiva,* 205). The celebration of being in the pampas, then, turns into something that was already accessible, but not yet fully perceived, for it exceeds mintage. There are always voices attesting to the insolvent character of currency, its inner frivolity—that we gently admit to and do not merely tolerate. It is rather curious that Espina himself claims "money has always been insolvent." (*Ema, la Cautiva,* 205). Yet, he blames this on quantity, "quantity itself is insolvent. The quantity of species in the world dissolves nature. The quantity of nature dissolves humanity" (*Ema, la Cautiva,* 205). Beyond Artaud's theater of cruelty, which demands that bodies be doubled in advance, Espina's monetary policy puts this request to double the bodies on the bills, "how could paper bills not be a cataclysm, if in them quantity is everything, and it is always almost multiplying itself? In European civilization sadism has restrained any transformation" (*Ema, la Cautiva,* 205).

Is cruelty sadism, or that which compels beings to double themselves? Is the default sadistic? Is it the other of any sadism? "The Indians invented the theater of money. As with its mechanisms, the theater of money has something that is contradictory: an indifferent sadism" (*Ema, la Cautiva,* 205), a sadism beyond repetition. What is it to be otherwise, but a different repetition [*repetición distinta*]? To what extent is being mirroring its (his)torizing in the pampas? "It seems to me," Espina says, "that the Indians are beyond the different repetition. They have reached the point where money accumulates and annihilates itself at the same time. We are so far from them ..." (*Ema, la Cautiva,* 205). Yet, it is Ema who finally makes the move toward something beyond mintage, something that remains undefined: *ποίησις,* poultry-breeding in the pampas, what had not been taking place yet but is about to. Is it casual that Aira finished the novel in the ruins of New Rome? Or is it a symbol of something that we will know soon? After a whole year of *ποίησις,* they found a place where "they carefully mottled their bodies. They sat down to smoke in the salon heading toward the bay, staring at the waves brought by the tempest, thinking or sleeping" (*Ema, la Cautiva,* 234).

Κουροτρόφος

You guide them to the developing dish, you let them lie down there until they heal. They may seem dead to you, but they will wake up, and with their radiance they will give you signs.

He healed the pictures, like any Apollonian priest. His body was a shield against the splendid and destructive radiance of the day. He let them lie still in darkness, until they began to cast their own radiance, their alien light into the day. By then, his limbs rested, and they surrounded him and healed him.

Creatures of light, incomplete forms, containing almost every being.

Quite often the reflected image resembled the form of a wanderer, the very same form that in June I found at Delphi.

For rendering Parmenides' poem you only need to look at the vase of the underworld painter. Yes, a crater from Apulia, one with an image of the underworld.

If you reflect your image in three mirrors, you will see your entire self, and yet something that may completely exceed its shape. It will also reflect once and for all everything that could happen to it, and all that it could be said of it.

When she asked about my future plans she avoided using "will." This is not because there is no such a thing as willingness, but because one is doing, and will do, what one has already been doing. That is what they call predetermination, conflagration, or extension. That is, undoubtedly, another monstrosity of the language, its many indulgences, its many exceptions, its congenial arbitrariness. One always keeps his or her mother language, for no one would bother to correct the travelers. Those who settled down during the construction of the railroad still use their language to ask for bread. It sounds / bræd / or / vrœd /, a very short, sharp sound indeed. There are several, uncountable names for anything (Cf. Parmenides, Fragments 8 and 9).

One may say that this is inventiveness, the richness of the language. From a distance, I believe it is quite the opposite. One and the same word means "to tell," "to count," "to foretell" (Cf. Aira, *The Hare*, 1–47). *To understand, then, is to witness, to cunningly persuade, or to be fully present when someone vanishes in the extension of the land or behind the mountains.*

ALTERATION AND TRADITION

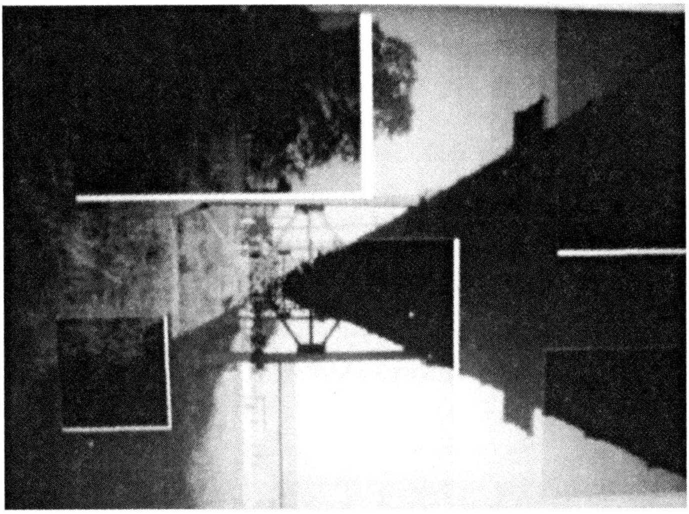

Those who claim that the peg led to recession come to forget that recession was already taking place in the pampas.* In its familiarity, recession exhibited itself as *ἄπειρον*, not only because one can not get through it, but because it was never thematized beyond the limits that temporality had set for it, that of mintage. Ontology in the pampas, indeed, did not make explicit this issue beyond the boundaries of philosophical anthropology, the question of the "Argentine character." The question of being in the pampas was displaced toward the very margins of philosophy, toward the frontier. As we saw in *Ema, la Cautiva,* literary writers addressed the question of being in the pampas in terms of *place* and in terms of *in,* but in doing so, they also faced the task of rethinking their position with regard to the Argentinean tradition, particularly with regard to the *gauchesco*

poetry to which the captive, New Rome, and the paradoxes of mintage belong.

What, it is asked, could be the place of any Argentine writer with regard to the tradition? What are the limits, the distances separating their authors and their themes? How to fill the void between these writers? What is the place of the captive, or the *gaucho* within this *in* of being in the pampas? *Place* itself is a notion that opens itself to a claim: being always exceeds itself, and dwells in its abundance, "it is greater than itself and less than itself." Yet in its inadequacy, being never fits in its own place.

It is a literary curiosity, *un hallazgo,* that Borges addressed this issue with a certain skepticism, a skepticism "not related to the difficulty or impossibility of resolving the problem, but to its very existence," for he found it "a rhetorical theme," "an appearance, a simulacrum, a pseudo-problem" (Borges, *Selected Non-Fictions,* 420).

From the point of view of temporal ontology, the bounds of Argentine literature "already exist in *gauchesco* poetry," but what temporality demands from the Argentine writer is that "the lexicon, techniques, and subject matter of the *gauchesco* poetry should enlighten the contemporary writer, and are a point of departure and perhaps an archetype" (*Selected Non-Fictions,* 420). Is this demand for the continuity of themes compatible in any sense with our demand for excess? Can being unfold itself in a Chinese novel written in the pampas? After following Aira's *Ema, la Cautiva,** we see how writers often exceed the solution proposed by Lugones in *El Payador,* that in the pampas there is a "a classic poem, *Martín Fierro,* and that this poem should be for us what the Homeric poems were for the Greeks" (*Selected Non-Fictions,* 420): a common place, full of gossip and interludes of ontological problems, and indeed, inexhaustible, taxable, *ἄπειρον.* Borges finds this temporal limit—taking *Martin Fíerro* as a sort of "Bible, our canonical book" (*Selected Non-Fictions,* 420)—an impossibility. Yet, being itself is impossible, for it exceeds temporality. We have to interpret Borges's reaction against the gaucho *bravucón* and *quejoso* depicted by Hernández as a way of moving away from tradition; or better, as a way of displaying that tradition always exceeds itself.

Borges points out the difficulties of temporal order, but not without a certain reticence. To claim that octosyllabic meter may ensure the continuum between the gauchos themselves (*payadores*), and the authors of *gauchesco* poetry so as to present a "continuation or derivation of the poetry of the gauchos. . . ." (*Selected Non-Fictions,* 421), is to forget and yet with remarkable exaggerations ensure that "the popular poets of the countryside and the outskirts of the city versify general themes: the pain of love and absence, the sorrow of love, and they do so in a lexicon that is equally general; the *gauchesco* poets, on the contrary, cultivate a deliberately popular language that the popular poets do not even attempt." One may notice in passing how in the many versions of the captive—the last are really monstrous, obscene constructions that I may not write on—"there is a quest for native words, a profusion of local color" (*Selected Non-Fictions,* 421) that makes them plainly artificial and yet excessive.

For this mimesis to take place, to give room—or even create a void—for exaggerations and retellings, one needs to consider that Hernández's "*Martín Fierro* is written in a *gauchesco*-accented Spanish, and for a long while the poem does not allow us to forget that the person singing it is a gaucho" (*Selected Non-Fictions,* 422), but also that the poem exercises cruelty upon itself, upon its characters, who switch from the vernacular, local color, to "great, abstract subjects: time, space, the sea, the night ... [in] the *payada,* the improvised musical face-off between Martín Fiero and El Moreno that occupies the end of the second part" (*Selected Non-Fictions,* 422). The scandal of the impossible: Martín Fierro discussing ontology in the pampas, incongruence in itself taking place as an imperative.

Nevertheless, within a temporal framework the boundaries for incongruence are set in such a way that temporality ensures that Argentine poetry must "abound in Argentine differential traits and in Argentine local color," exaggerating them to a remarkable degree, turning them almost invisible. What Borges finds misleading—or rather, a mistake—is to think that Martín Fierro is more (or less) incongruous than Blanch's poem *La urna.* Confronted with the disjunctive, which book is more Argentine, *Martín Fierro* or the sonnets in *La urna*? Borges finds no convincing arguments "to say that the former is more Argentine." Further, Borges finds that the latter may be more Argentinean—that is, in a way that the book exceeds Argentinean traits—for "in Blanchs's *La urna* there are neither Argentine landscapes, nor Argentine topography, nor Argentine botany, nor Argentine zoology; nevertheless, there are other specifically Argentine conditions in *La urna*" (*Selected Non-Fictions,* 422).

What does it mean to write a line such as "the sun glints on the tiled roofs and on the windows" in the pampas? Where does the *in*, the Argentinean character reside? "Enrique Blanch," says Borges, "wrote these lines in a house on the edge of Buenos Aires, and on the edges of Buenos Aires there are no tiled roofs, there are flat, terrace roofs." Incongruency offers itself as a continuum, as excess of being. Again "nightingales mean to say they are in love" already presupposes the *ἄπειρον* condition of what is said, "the nightingale is not so much a real bird as a bird of literature, of the Greek and Germanic tradition." What is taking place is incongruence in itself, "in these *incongruous* tiled roofs and nightingales" one is supposed to find—visible and fully present as being—"the Argentine reserve, the Argentine reticence," a certain wariness "significant of the difficulty we have in confiding, in being intimate" (*Selected Non-Fictions*, 423). Besides his incongruent digression on Argentinean character, Borges demands that Argentinean literature be incongruous: a literature that acknowledges the excess that exceeds its place, that does not fear to take, to welcome sources, extravagant quotations, monstrous metaphors, Homeric lines, sounds, images taken from the *Suda*, or borrowed from a German saga (Audhumbla the cow, almost certainly; Odin or Wotan, perhaps, but not the dwarfs and the forest); in brief, that goes beyond the nationalist boundaries imposed by temporality, which sets literary limits within "differential traits of the country." There is only one addition made to this thesis on literature: opening the space for events to take place, for believing in being in the pampas "*without abounding in local color*" (*Selected Non-Fictions*, 423, italics added), and perhaps, vice-versa. Isn't Estanislao del Campo's *Fausto* excessive? What does it mean to posit a gaucho in a theatre, watching a performance of the *Fausto*? Does this performance lead to a glimpse of the default of being?

The problem of the discontinuity of the territory is not of thinking a territory within time, but that of thinking a territory that is "more than itself and less than itself." It has been noted that in his thematizing of being in Velia—that of not cutting off from being what is in being—Parmenides used Homeric imagery. But we can also imagine that he could find it unconceivable to "only speak of neighborhoods and ranches and not of the universe" (*Selected Non-Fictions*, 424). Indeed, as long as we are talking of the universe, we are already displaying our dwelling in ranches, fully depreciated, living the hyperinflation of being.

Borges also perceives the danger of cutting ourselves off from being, of holding onto "the opinion that we Argentines are cut off from the past; that there has been some sort of rupture between ourselves and Europe" (*Selected Non-Fictions*, 425). Unless we acknowledge the *ἄπειρον* character of being, this issue will never be straightened out: "according to this singular point of view, we Argentines are as if in the first days of creation; our search for European subject matters and techniques is an illusion, an error; we must understand that we are essentially alone, and cannot play at being European" (*Selected Non-Fictions*, 425); the temporal fallacy of a "first, primordial event" is always deferred.

Yet Borges has been vituperated for his opinion that Argentineans belong to the "whole of Western culture" for he repeatedly opposed what he saw as European culture against barbarism, expressed in binary polarities: cosmopolitan (or Western)/nationalist, civilized/barbarian, citizen/gaucho or Indian. To milk a cow without revering Audhumbla is already a way of acting. This contempt can be made explicit as follows: What does it mean to "act within that culture and at the same time not feel bound to it by any special devotion" (*Selected Non-Fictions*, 426)? Besides, aren't the gaucho, the captive, all of us already acting in this way? What is innovation in being but "a mere affection, a mask" (*Selected Non-Fictions*, 427).

It could be misleading to point out that Borges's understanding of the tradition is already within a temporal conception of being. We need to make the effort to read his work as setting the very limits of temporal ontology. The same Borges who is primarily concerned about time can claim that once we deny matter and mind, which are continuities, we may not have any claim over time. Indeed, Borges has a tendency to underestimate the value of space, and to thematize metaphysical questions within the boundaries of time, assigning to it succession and the connection of images. One may glimpse this tendency toward excess in Borges's thought by looking at the resoluteness of his ontological inquiry. "The classic postulation of reality can take three forms, which are quite diversely accessible. The easiest consists of a general notification of the important facts.... The second consists of imagining a more complex reality than the one declared to the reader and describing its derivations and results" (*Selected Non-*

Fictions, 62). Borges places ontology in the third one, "The third method, the most difficult and effective of them all, makes use of the *invention of circumstances* ... which makes frequent use of no other procedure than an unfolding series of those laconic details with broad implications" (*Selected Non-Fictions*, 63).

The use of this third method—the invention of circumstances—has been posited in advance as a way of ensuring the continuum of being in the pampas. This is the case at least in two senses: (i) Humor, the put-on, makes extensive use of invention as a way of dealing with a reality already set up within temporal boundaries; and (ii) ontology includes it as a way of dealing with the lack of sources, and for thematizing the problem of traits or "national character" that are also bounded by temporality. Undoubtedly, both of these converge in their rejection of the idea that philosophy in the pampas needs to go to school, and for a long time. Humor, for instance, posits that philosophers have already gone to school, but after their commencement they find the fallacies, or rather, the futility behind those onerous years of study. The ontology unfolded by humor, on the other hand, is one of cruelty—in the sense of doubling the bodies: laughter convulses the body and puts it in proximity to danger, close to *κόρος*.

Thus, Macedonio's works persistently make a theme of the author, and question whether such an author is really qualified (in terms of Borges's credentials) to write what he or she already is writing. What, or rather who entitles Macedonio to write an ontological work such as "A crippled man's guide to the proper way of living?" (Cf. Fernández, *Museo de la Novela de la Eterna*, 3). If temporality demands that the author be a serious scholar, Macedonio shows that this is temporality's requirement. His allusions to his instructive "temperament," his insistence on the fact that he has *really* read Kant and Bergson—or at least, that he "writes about" them frequently—are examples of his will to be a metaphysician in the Río de la Plata.

Further, the put-on works as a reversal, showing a certain reticence, as an all-inclusive campaign for the presidency of the pampas, for continuity itself. In any display of being, we should proceed by "giving to it the appearance of having an affair of the heart ... this sort of thing: Macedonio is looking for Casilda, the Cuban. Please call Rivadavia 3729" (Englebert, *Macedonio Fernández and the Spanish*

American New Novel, 41). Continuity is granted by further retellings, by wandering, two-headed, dazed tribes, by acting out a novel "in the streets of Buenos Aires, in homes, in restaurants, etc.—a novel (or at least important scenes of one, making the public believe that it is really taking place)" (*Macedonio Fernández and the Spanish American New Novel,* 43).

Indeed, it would be misleading to read Macedonio's works as allegories, unless we understand that allegories themselves exceed their being *ἄλλεν,* and their being bounded by time. As with Borges, the implications are broad and not necessarily explicit. Yet, an implication may, or perhaps has to, be forgotten in order to exceed itself. Forgetting is not only a way to overlook, but also an expression of how difficult it is to keep the reader awake concerning the political as such. How did Irigoyen "defeat" Macedonio? (Cf. Engelbert, *Macedonio Fernández and the Spanish American New Novel,* 43). By how many votes? What is a captive vote? From a literary point of view, Macedonio's project reveals the demands imposed on the Argentine writer by temporality: (i) to be a fierce authority rather than an unknown; (ii) to have attended private school, at least up until nine years old; (iii) to have a brother or sister who can read and understand Bergson's philosophical writings, something that the author may not achieve, not even with all the intelligence that the author's wealthy family may afford (Cf. *Museo,* 6); (iv) to quote masterfully, confronted by the scandal of admitting "I haven't read Bergson, but I write about him quite frequently, as these pages show" (Cf. *Museo,* 6).

What Macedonio makes explicit is that doxography is a demand imposed by temporality on ontology, a demand that ontology itself may not be able to fulfill, because ontology does not rely on time, but on *place.* Ontology is the addition of monstrous details to a biographical note, is a retelling that "belong(s) to the kind of things that we do not know about [a certain author]" (Cf. *Museo,* 3). Its additions, emendations, deletions are manifest proof in abundance of a surfeit that is necessary in order to fill an existence whose contents are unknown, and yet if we could not know something else about the author we could also make it public (Cf. *Museo,* 3). Like Diogenes Laertius, or Galen before, Macedonio published "an irritating book to read: with its come-ons, its put-ons, its run-arounds, it will tease the reader as he's never been teased before but suppress his reflex to stop reading" (*Macedonio: Selected Writings in Translation,* 82).

In defying chronology itself, Macedonio exhibits ontology as that within which Mark Twain, Sterne, and Gomez de la Serna appear as good friends, and "*criollos,*" who attempted to become contemporaries of each other in order to see each other more frequently (Cf. *Museo,* 3). As for the reader—the jump-around reader—such a reader is confronted with Macedonio's unfolding of being in the pampas by "a jump-around author, [who] tried so hard to trick you into imagining that you were an orderly reader that you were actually made to doubt the stability of the identity of your jump-around self" (*Macedonio: Selected Writings in Translation,* 84). The prologues to the pampas are, then, justified as taking place and giving place. In this giving place, in this transference of functions one can glimpse the radical movement that took place in the prose of Borges and Aira: the continuum in which the author finds himself asleep in paroxysms when the writing doesn't move on except through being's unfolding as *siesta* (Cf. *Museo,* 11.) This is not a return to a certain "ethics of reader's response," according to which the temporal reactions of readers—their convulsive contortions, their desire to print the bill by using the paperback, their obsession with futurist fashion—matter as influences, as "controlling" the text.* When speaking of excess we have made clear that this excess is produced by currency, images, fashion, and signs *by themselves,* and that they establish a continuum by themselves, by their weaknesses, by their many lines, saying too much and nothing at all (Cf. *Museo,* 15).

Besides, the continuum is granted by the reader, any reader (a hare, the captive, Drucfoult, Rosas, a dog), "so today anybody can have that distinction and go down in history as the first reader of you-know-which author. When I think about how my book, *Not All Waking Consciousness Is the Open-eyed Variety,* that's the only good thing that I can see that it will probably do" (*Macedonio Fernández: Selected Writings in Translation,* 39), but this idea is difficult to grasp except as a cruel excess upon and by the reader, a cruelty that "culminates in the use of incongruities, to the point of forgetting all about the identity of the characters and their continuity along with such things as temporal sequences and causes before effect, etc." (*Macedonio Fernández: Selected Writings in Translation,* 86). This carrying along—by much-guided mares—offers what Macedonio called "emotional impetus" (*Macedonio Fernández: Selected Writings in Translation*, 86).

Macedonio objects to temporality, to its temporal framework (*Gestell*), claiming that it is not suitable for addressing the question of being in the pampas. Photographic images, for instance, cannot be thought of as mere representations or likenesses of reality, but rather as the excess of reality, as *ἄπειρον*. Macedonio finds himself caught up in the task of resembling his portrait, unsuccessfully trying for fifteen years to look like it, until he discovers that his face, now somehow clumsy, is a semblance of the picture (Cf. *Museo*, 21)—something that can only be compared to the difficulties involved in taking a photograph that resembles a face with fidelity (Cf. *Museo*, 21). Indeed, this excess in the similarity between the photograph and the face is dissolved into a continuum that takes place and goes beyond its own frame. The similitude consists in the dispersion, in the excesses that the photograph offers; for within temporality one may understand photography in terms of not exceeding one's place, "A good portrait does not express a character but a single moment of one from which nothing can be inferred about the character as a whole, because the *congruence* of individual character is a senseless concept: from no trait is it possible to infer any other (and the same could be said about the Cosmos, about all Reality)" (Engelbert, *Macedonio Fernández and the Spanish American New Novel*, 154–155). Indeed, the question that Macedonio poses remains without an answer: Who is going to deny one's resemblance to one's own portraits? (Cf. *Museo*, 21).

Photographic images, indeed, give us clues as to how Macedonio thematized the continuum in writing. To enframe means to exceed the frame, to write means to exceed the written. A photographic image discloses the tendency of being to go beyond its own boundaries, going beyond itself in such a way that proliferation always takes place. Moreover, if the problem of the continuum is to be unfolded in the excess produced by motion and stillness, it should be made explicit in the futility of cutting off what is in being from holding fast to what is in being, by means of a cut that produces this excess—something that was already advanced by fashion, whose cut always exceeds the mere cutting off. An expression such as Macedonio's "Last night I ..." unfolds the surfeit of being by using the continuum itself. Similarly, an expression such as "Being in the pampas I ..." may bring the collapse of necessity as if it could take off, vanish (Cf. Aira, *The Hare,* 39). Naturally, this commotion is still feasible in the pampas, no less than its other: a new tax, a doll hanging askew on a rancho's wall, time.... And it is within this closeness that a tendency toward minimalism is fully expressed. Futurist gauchos will prefer jokes without context, metaphors without context, and even passion without context, to temporal constructions using *haber.* Yet, to ensure a minimal continuum books written in prose will be extremely brief, a fragment with only one line (Cf. *Museo,* 22).

Minimalism, the authentication of non-doing, the invention of circumstances, are ways of dealing with the problem of the continuum within and exceeding recession, underproduction, and overconsumption that we have pointed out with regard to mintage. Mixing, mingling, unfolding, deleting, interpreting, adding, taking from its context all take place as a prototype of ontology within which the entries in a foreman's journal, the recollections of a cook or a supplier, and some pages taken from a novel may be seen as a model of continuity (Cf. *Museo,* 23). This paradox, the continuum grounded in *la autenticación del No-hacer* is indeed to be thematized within *place.*

Further, within ontology, this inventiveness is manifested by the ever-growing, hyperinflated nature of a squash that is to replace being itself. Macedonio conceives that being is immersed in a squash that grows in size to the point that that it includes the country and the universe in its process of expansion, in its process of going beyond its "natural" limits, to the point that the politics of mintage as such—the Argentinean "living in a squash" *vivir dentro de un zapallo*—is expressed as "so ridiculous and humiliating, putting oneself inside it so precipitously—one might forget one's watch or hat, or leave a cigarette burning somewhere—but there is no longer a world outside of the Squash" (*Macedonio Fernández: Selected Writings in Translation,* 56). Once immersed in it, "we devoutly practice Cucurbitaceous Metaphysics. We are now convinced that, given the relativity of all magnitudes, none of us will ever know whether or not we live inside a squash.... It had to happen: a wholly internal Totality, Bounded, Immobile (without Change), without external Relationships, thus without death" (*Macedonio Fernández: Selected Writings in Translation,* 57). The crisis, the recession, the default of being that minimalism reveals demands more and more place, "it appears that in these latest moments, according to the signs, the Squash gets ready to conquer not just the poor Earth, but the Creation. Evidently, it prepares to challenge the Milky Way. In a few days, the Squash will be Being, Reality and its Shell" (*Macedonio Fernández: Selected Writings in Translation*, 57).

Within the hyperinflation of being—or rather, of the squash—*ἄπειρον* is exhibited as the cycles of lives that anyone is compelled to live. The crisis of the university, for instance, will not to be understood unless interruption is thought as part of it. Its delays, its detours, its incongruities, its futile digressions are part of our character. And yet, in the pampas, "all the characters are under contract *to dream of being*, which is their unique propensity, a state of mind unattainable by the living and the only genuine matter of Art. To be a character is to be real" (Engelbert, *Macedonio Fernández and the Spanish American New Novel*, 156). What is called interruption, damage, couture, or Lethe is a sort of trance in which one weaves what one was trying to say together with the "thread" of other topics. The continuum is ensured by surfeit, by trying on the perfect congruency that the speaker's tone has woven. This continuity, or rather, the discontinuity that ensures the continuum, takes place within a crisis, a default that shows how temporal statements are indefinite in their time reference except by their tone, by the *entonación fonética grande, perfecta* (Cf. *Museo*, 30). Laughter, then, exceeds its being the deformation of the face and its belonging to the put-on, to the political reality as such, to the unconcealment such that "bulb smuggling carries the death penalty" (Aira, *The Hare*, 187). Once the continuum is ensured by writing itself—as minimalist, as digressive—it finds expression in the many signs, quotations, references, sources, oblivion that prevent the cutting off from reality by postulating that any failure to fulfill a payment is impossible, that "the only intelligible cessation will end Everything; the private end of someone who has once felt ceasing to feel while the rest of reality remains unchanged is a verbal contradiction, an impossible conception" (*Macedonio Fernández: Selected Writings in Translation*, 69).

Furthermore, this failure to fulfill payments due was already taking place before the default. Minimalism only ensures "a way out of" by means of something primordial that does not rule out the possibility that a multiplicity of characteristics of being in the pampas may be constitutive of the *in*. Thus, in asking the question of being in the pampas we turn toward a radical path that ensures the payment of what is due and exceeds the payment itself. Minimalism reveals that any mere monetary policy remains within "the equal possibility of nothingness and being, and he believed the intelligible and possible substitution of all-being by all-nothing" (*Macedonio Fernández: Selected Writings in Translation*, 72). Moreover, granted the possibility of exchange—the peg between dollars and pesos in the exchange rate switchboards, visible by everyone—a substitution, *el canje* becomes crucial, and yet irrelevant to determine the character of being, for what is taking place there is also holding fast to what is taking place here, "if World or Nothingness are of absolutely equal possibility, then in this scale or balance of Being or Nothingness a thread, a drop of dew, a sigh, a wish, an idea, can be enough to precipitate the change from a World of Being to one of Non-Being" (*Macedonio Fernández: Selected Writings in Translation*, 72). Yet *ποίησις* remains hidden as "a Fact," "a fact that humiliates and horrifies the Secret (being / Mystery) is the martyrdom of Vegetable Innocence by the highest personalization of Consciousness, the highest non-mechanical power: Man. Such a deed, without need of verification, merely conceived by a human consciousness, I believe could shake everything that exists toward Non-Being" (Macedonio, 1984: 73).

Ultimately, this process of inventing circumstances, and reducing them to a minimal and digressive (hi)story, is already displayed by rumors, retellings, idle-talk, the uncontrolled murderous violence of a chorus that disperses the text in many directions, tracing many paths. It is in this way that both the events of New Rome and the events that precipitated the default are to be understood. Equally, Macedonio was compelled to give his place to the reader, "now I turn over the pen to the reader so that he/she can depict for him/herself what I could not possibly describe: the madness, the fear, the terror, the futile efforts to get free as the guards drag him along, the horror of being seated on that chair and having his hands strapped down" (Macedonio, 1984: 62). Naturally, this is already cruelty—doubling the author—but Macedonio expects it to suffice to ontologically exhibit the character of the continuum, as long as the reader is in charge of an exigency that is to be exceeded, that of believing in the continuity of the story, that of reaching mystic awareness (Cf. Fernández, *Museo de la Novela de la Eterna*, 41).

If we take this gesture as a convulsive reply to doxography, as a way of historizing ontology by giving the rumors beforehand, what is revealed is, again, the inattentive character of *κόρος* or excess. Ontology may provoke "the sudden convulsions of laughter" by its many footnotes, digressions, parentheses; these ensure the continuity of the story because they mirror incongruence (Cf. *Museo*, 41). Censorship in the pampas, then, is explicated, defined in terms of excess, a surfeit where the "and" and the "then" turn every sequence of words into a narrative (Cf. *Museo*, 42).

We may counter this gesture with the default, this recounting as a common tragedy in the pampas, this retelling of the depreciation of being, to the discontinuity of the territory. Tragedy is a politico-literary affair, a living novel that mimics itself and the universe. The attorney Macedonio Fernández is already the author of the poems Macedonio Fernández will dismiss years later. The default can only be matched by disinheritance—*la desherencia*. "The century which is to abolish inheritance will itself inherit hardly anything" (Engelbert, *Macedonio Fernández and the Spanish American New Novel*, 12). Is the hyperinflation of being the daughter of inheritance? Is it a daughter? A tear? A superstition? "a single thought of herself?" (*Macedonio Fernández and the Spanish American New Novel*, 5). Retellings of tragedy then, seem to be a preliminary to a representation of tragedy, a prelude even to something that is not yet taking place, as if the only expectation that tragedy may produce is delayed in a deferral in a given time. The tragic character of tragedy is the lack of plenitude or fulfillment of what is taking place or of that which cannot take place, which is veiled. Macedonio characterizes it by means of an unfulfilled love (Cf. *Museo*, 50) that depends on a balance among death, forgetfulness, and love, but it's not easy to balance such a budget. Tragedy is defined by this lack of accomplishment of what must take place, of what is not taking place in the pampas yet. Can we pay the interest on the debt? Can we pay the debt with interest?

Temporality demands that ontology be written within this deferral. Macedonio, indeed, accomplished the task of writing a book full of repetitions, digressions, emendations, rejections, contradictions, regresses *ad infinitum* in order to display being in the pampas. Further, Macedonio shows how temporality, the deferral, turns metaphysicians into privileged subjects who have the opportunity to write a second book on the same topic, in order to censor, contradict, or rectify the former text, a task that demands a rigorous decision in the selection of a title (Cf. *Museo,* 54). From the possible excessive titles that may sound accurate in the pampas, Macedonio chose the title "Psychology of an equestrian statue's horse," leaving aside such titles as "Metaphysics of an experimental God," "A God with astonishment at being," "Metaphysics of a statue of Condillac with astonishment at being."

Dreams, Macedonio goes on to claim, display the intensity that he demands of reality, of being in the pampas. The bureaucracy of being in the pampas is replaced by a "mystic state ... to live as if uncreated and self-subsistent" (Englelbert, *Macedonio Fernández and the Spanish American New Novel,* 85). Does this state abolish the distinction between images and perceptions, dream and reality, the collapse of being and its *ἐπιφαινόμενον*? How can we sleep over it while in default? Yet "being, is one, continuous, selfless and substantial and utterly knowable. Being *is* because it is a Dream, that is, an immediate plenitude" (*Macedonio Fernández: Selected Writings in Translation,* 26). Do dreams exhibit vivacity, can one claim that our life in the pampas is beyond tears? Is the political as such unbounded by images that exceed spatial and temporal causality? Causality must exceed itself, it must include the unexpected as a cause; causing fuss by being irrelevant, and by its complete lack of interest to anyone (Cf. Aira, *The Hare,* 33).

The activity of the *siesta* is now fully explicit. Hegel once observed how the aboriginals of the pampas spent their time in forty winks. We have tried to show that *siesta*—stillness, *ἡσυχία*—can also be conceived as the unconcealment of being in the pampas, as long as *siesta* itself exceeds its boundaries. To paraphrase Macedonio, dreams that take place when we are asleep do not differ from the dreams, thoughts, images, memories, and oblivions we have when we are awake (*Museo,* 111). The question of being in the pampas exceeds itself as many other questions. How do dreams exceed themselves? In what images? What is the relationship between *κόρος* and *sueño*?

Being in the pampas, as Macedonio displays it, is being immersed in a dream that exceeds its dreamlike boundaries, in a hyperinflated dream. While ontology insists on claiming that a phenomenon is circumscribed in its place, assigned to its real place, Macedonio's ontology manifests the excess, the intensity—the mystical category—of the real. That is as far as the real must go in its resemblance to dreams. The image of Hobbes in the pampas may appear dream-like; and indeed, it exhibits the need for ontology in the pampas. Temporality has restrained this way of doing ontology by silencing voices, the chorus, the rumors, putting order into phenomena, categorizing "in time," in "agreement with time," perhaps ensuring that the regress *ad infinitum* conceived by the Eleatic thinkers would never take place, and the "chronology" and "doxography" inherent in any fragment would never take place. Excess, *ἄπειρον*, is then to be put aside into the margins of philosophy. Sets of rules, categories, principles, axioms, are expected to make explicit their foundations. This is manifest in the primacy of signs as an ontological theme.

Family Pictures

It is only by driving her Citroën that Nora becomes Persephone.

The first thing that I noticed about the Libertador had to do with his soldiers, for all of them died in exile. And none of these gauchos were aware of it. He swept it under the pampas, that carpet. Once he told them a joke. That he only wanted to flee from the plain lands. Naturally, no one believed him, for this thought must have seemed senseless to the gauchos, so used were they to the pampas. Every one of them fought in the fields of Chacabuco and at the gates of Lima. They did not realize that they were carried away. For the first time, they saw the mountains and what lies behind the mountains. They left behind their cards, their dogs, and that abstract thing, the fatherland. They learned how to leave behind what we now teach in high school. The same cruelty, under the same laws, and nothing else.

Later I included in the script the figures that most resembled the Libertador. I spent a lot of time working on the unity of the plot until the day when the students, and their mothers who volunteered for the play, abolished the stage and the auditorium (Artaud, *The Theatre and Its Double*, 78). *They also insisted on decorating the stage with flags and vases that they filled with oil and cruelty. In one of the scenes, the Libertador sank the Graf Spee with all its crew into the muddy waters of the Río de la Plata. Those who swam to shore never left the land. He also killed the natives who lived on the shore of the river, and ate their flesh. That was, of course, the reversal of the image in the portrait. The absolute other. Extension.*

They also asked me to represent him as a female goddess, filling their dresses with huge fake breasts to represent him, the ones who by definition kept male apart from female (Parmenides, Fragment 17).

Only six of his soldiers came back to the pampas. A whim? A well-thought-out action? It is useless to ask. The rest of them, by dying or mating, remained in foreign lands. It is like an equation ... body = limbs = thought. Since their limbs think, and those limbs wander much.... (Parmenides, Fragment 16) *But nothing about this will ever be said.*

It is in that room where I finished the translation or perhaps I abandoned the task at some point.

That last scene made a strong impression on Nora, for she was brought up on a farm. Driving tractors during the harvest, herding horses, branding cows, preparing the mate. *No small matters, no. It is precisely because of that education that she became so caring, so maternal. Sometimes, indeed, she burst out for no reason. Loudly. Full of cruelty, her mouth, for she was cruel to a remarkable degree. She asked me to play the guitar, the goddess, and then she danced among the children, adding more confusion to the already disarranged play. Those were the days after a depreciation. Nothing, absolutely nothing could be denied in those days.*

During the depreciation one lives day by day, as in a daydream. One accepts and loves these cycles with erotic desires. One also gets old, and more or less dies at the age of seventeen just to be born again at the age of thirty. After several cycles, whose number has been forbidden to write, one can see everything between light and shadow, and things seem to be one, if not the same.

The family photos are finally emerging from the developing dish. I took them in Harding Green. A job that I took in exchange for food. I was one of the very few who could still gain access to Harding Green, for they have blocked the main gate with bricks. They do not allow anyone to get into their villa and see how wretched they are. Inside their mansions, they play old songs and have dinner in the early afternoon. They pretend not to understand what happened to them. They believe that someday somehow someone will visit them. That is why they try to keep the garden and the house so neat, and their daughters single. They hire servants they can not afford. At night, they beat their wives because the railroad does not run anymore. Because they could not flee from an untamed land. Slowly, gradually, they are becoming part of the pampas. Extension. *It will be as simple as this, they will cease painting the house, and then the ceiling will fall. Next, the curtains will get yellow, and the clothes old. For now they close the gate with bricks, because they are still afraid of being confused with the beggars and their dogs. They are two headed, they do not understand that the pampas are complete. They are already immersed in them, and not only at their lintel.*

They write letters to their families on the islands, hoping against hope. I spent many afternoons drinking their rum and looking into their icy eyes. One day they trusted me with the job of photographing their children. Each one of them, any one of them reminds me of Octavio, "Tavito." He also was the son of a man of the railroad, and his family was wealthy on the farm. When his parents died, he didn't know what to do with his wealth, so he spent it all. One day he did not have anything left. His relatives tried to help him out twice, I think, but it was my grandfather who finally lent him money. Being unable to go back to the islands, he lived in a small brick room that he used as a bedroom, kitchen, bathroom and library, a yellow room with only one window. He used to play guitar and think out loud for hours. Once his relatives came to visit him and gave him money that he rejected with pride. And he told them that it is also possible to live in poverty. He did not know how much he had already become part of the land. For four years he tried to keep his word or to prove its truth. But finally he gave up his thesis. He committed double suicide by shooting at his head and by hanging from a barbed wire. And he did not fail. My grandfather almost bought his guitar for me, but my grandmother refused.

ASSERTIONS

Such an assertion as "the State is hyperinflated" not only echoes "being is hyperinflated," but also Macedonio's own assertions on the inflation of the State, which Fernández Latour recalls: "He had a horror of giantism and of bureaucratic red tape and the increasingly restrictive legislation curtailing the rights of the individual" (quoted in Engelbert, *Macedonio Fernández and the Spanish American New Novel,* 12). What is difficult to understand is the "pointing out" that a temporal ontology grounded on the before and after demands of such an assertion; and not because it is imprecise, vague, but because it insists on unveiling with excess what is visible for the most part and consequently concealed by mintage. Such an assertion already brings in images from the beginning (i.e., looting, the riots, forms of cruelty that repeat themselves and do not double the bodies). Within it, and beyond it, the default is made explicit in advance. It is already taking place in the pampas because we have promoted the tendency toward, the march down to the inflation of the State, the curtailing of individual rights that eventually made savings, retirements, life itself vanish (Cf. Fernández, *Museo de las Novela de la Eterna,* 375). Indeed, such an assertion may equally mean that "the state is taking more place that itself" or that it is less than itself, almost a void.

When discussing the hyperinflation of the State it is easy to be led to an infinite regress; yet this regress *ad infinitum* should not be avoided, for it unfolds the very taking place of mintage. We may speculate whether the main role of the State is to exercise some sort of cruelty—the doubling of bodies compelling them to be fashionable, futurist, minimalist—or whether it leads to forms of asceticism and denials of *κόρος*. This has already been pointed out by Aira's thematizing of the individual right to mint one's own coins. Yet, his assertions are not to be read literally, but as a form of humor that illuminates, unconceals what is hidden for the most part by mintage (*ποίησις*, the question of the *respaldo*).

Heidegger articulated such an interpretation when he pointed out that "prior to all analysis, logic has already understood 'logically' what it takes as a theme under the heading of the 'categorical statement'" (Heidegger, *Being and Time*, 200). The statement "the State is hyperinflated" is temporally understood as that "This thing—the Argentine State" has a property, that of "being hyperinflated" in the pampas. Heidegger goes on to develop a theory of "concernful circumspection" according to which circumspection must display ways of exceeding any interpreting beforehand; and that is precisely what temporality does not always make manifest. To say "the State is hyperinflated," or even "Being is hyperinflated," is not only to make a still "theoretical judgment," but to emphasize the unbearable condition, the burden of being "hyperinflated" by pointing out what is not taking place. In this sense, Heidegger points out that the interpretation of such an assertion "is carried out primordially not in a theoretical statement but in an action of circumspective concern by laying aside the 'unsuitable' tool or exchanging it, 'without wasting words'" (*Being and Time*, 200).

Being in the pampas, then, already prefigures the inexhaustibility of any assertion as the means for granting the continuum; but the concept of "inexhaustibility" remains unintelligible unless we conceive that it surpasses every logical connection or linking that takes place with regard to reality. This is what Ross has thematized in *The Limits of Language* with regard to the very question of being: assertion, what is to passed out by gossip, by ontology, is excessive, always displaying a tendency toward regress *ad infinitum* (Cf. Ross, *The Limits of Language*, 83–101). Time adds nothing to this inexhaustibility unless time also exceeds itself, in such a way that it grants the continuum as taking place in the pampas. The captive, then, can be thematized as a captive woman, as a boy lost in Junin, as a Huiliche boy, or as every one of us with or without our savings. The paradox of the captive calls for an interpretation in terms of *ἄπειρον*: the captive always exceeds herself (*ποίησις* is only one of its forms); the story is inexhaustible in its many versions.

Furthermore, if assertions are to be thought with regard to the *is*, to the copula or bonding of a subject and predicate (the State and its hyperinflation, the gaucho and its futuristics, the captive, Ema, becoming a poultry-breeder), then the copula can not be *ὅρος*, can not be the limit for reaching conclusions. That is the aspect that Aristotle did not explicate with regard to his theory of the syllogism. Why did he call limit—*ὅρος*—the premise of any valid reasoning in the transition from the *Prior Analytics* to the *Posterior Analytics*? How can we understand this concept of *ὅρος* in the unlimited pampas? How is this conception related to time itself? The phenomenon of the copula is to remain hidden until we admit that its definition as the *bond* of a subject and a predicate depends on the limited character of which is asserted, and that this character has been regarded as self-evident by traditional ontology. But this relating that the copula is may obscure the further retellings that are taking place here and there, and that have been thematized by Eleatic thinkers as the concern of ontology itself. Heidegger rightly pointed out that "the term 'copula' has nothing to do with a bond or binding" (*Being and Time,* 202) but with being-there, with *Dasein* itself. However, we should not infer from this the task of building up some sort of existential analytic of the Argentinean traits that may also bind, limit the *κόρος*, the *ἄπειρον* being in the pampas.

This is exemplified by the way Argentinean writers have dealt with Rosas, the paradigm of rumor, the tyrant, the Restorer of Law, the captive. Rosas is magnified by the images of horror, of arbitrariness of forced exile in Banda Oriental, the fight against Anglo-French imperialism, Manuelita. Gossip, further retellings manifest the excess, the *ἄπειρον* and incongruous events related to Rosas. The tyrant who found refuge in England, the complexion of his face contrasting with his *gauchescho* manners, the apparatus and his dictionaries, the *rojo punzó* as fashion, the *mazorca* already prefiguring bureaucracy displaying "the secret man [who] came out into the light of day," and unconcealed for us an (un)fashionable man, "flabby, overweight, he was the color of wax and could not speak above a low voice. He never got back his confiscated lands; I think he died in poverty" (*In Praise of Darkness,* 65). Borges shows that the destiny of one, of Pedro Salvadores, is already installed as a "symbol of something that we are about to understand, but never quite do" (*In Praise of Darkness,* 65). These experiences preserved by gossip constitute both a fore-conception and ontology itself. Yet, their intelligibility is articulated as *ἄπειρον,* as exceeding the images that are to be to thought by means of interpretation and assertion. In this sense, the meaning of any assertion is inexhaustible. Don't we find its echoes in that assertion of Borges: "The government had confiscated his land; it was never returned to him. I believe he died in poverty. We see the fate of Pedro Salvadores, like all things, as a symbol of something that we are on the verge of understanding . . ." (Borges, *Collected Fictions*, 337).

GESTURES

Like the pampas, the poem is equal to itself from every direction.

I do not quite remember how the foreign exchange houses looked at that time. I remember the decoration: mirrors, chandeliers, useless armchairs, but I am unable to recall any particular face, perhaps because I have seen none. The clerks' desks were invariably covered by a mirror-glass. I only recall my face when asking to exchange my stipend for American dollars, my left hand inserting the bills in the revolving tray, and the dim light of an indicator board showing the exchange rate right behind my back. I only recall its inverted image. And my despair next to it.

Naturally, one can always talk to the "little trees." They are always waiting around the corner. But I should remind you, sometimes they do not come back with your money.

In any case, in those days I spent my time listening to the radio, like everyone else. Nora was the only one who didn't. I don't know how she managed to stay clear of money concerns. She enjoyed life like no one else. Perhaps because, after all, that was her underworld. There, she was Persephone. Driving her Citroën, playing with her dogs, shouting at some student. Those little things might still keep her going. She smoked most of the time, and she didn't say a word about exchange rates. That gained for her an exaggerated renown among the students. She had her savings, don't misunderstand me. But she also knew that we had never seen other things. Just alteration. Alteration, and new coins. Some of them were always turning around in her phonograph.

I didn't have news from her after I left the Bahía. She was brought up on a farm and she might have returned to it after she retired. She fed cows all her life, she told me once. And she had a pretty good theory about children and cows. One day, Nora took all the exams and become a high school principal. According to her, she was the Libertador. Twice.

Many crabs wounded his feet when he tried to push the car out of the shallows. From inside the car she asked him how many were many, and then they started laughing at each other. That was precisely the root of their friendship, to feel equally rooted in water.

After several rehearsals the students learned the gestures, the precise, punctual language and contortions necessary for the play. Some of the scenes were extremely demanding on their bodies, and we could not repeat them more than once a day. Sometimes, new gestures appeared on the Libertador's face, independent of any particular psychological use (Cf. Artaud, *The Theater and Its Double*, 94).

One needed to create his story every winter. Like a newborn, Persephone. I was strictly following my translation of Parmenide's poem when I wrote the plot. For his speech addressing the soldiers I used ἀλήθεια. *They begged me to replace* εἶναι *by* "Libertador." *His gracious solitude, his nostalgic cruelty, his insatiable indifference....*

He did not flee from the pampas, he was carried away.

Since most of the teachers didn't have a place to stay, they moved into the high school. During those days, they not only taught. They brought with them entertainment, food, and justice.

I let the students play with make up. Yes, both boys and girls. Despair seems to go away when one tries on someone else's clothes. Like the hide of the Minotaur.

At night they gathered at the shore and sang the national anthem and other songs, changing their lyrics in the most obscene or absurd way while beating their breasts and tearing their clothes apart, perhaps believing that in that way they would attract the attention of the passenger liners. These avoided the harbor. They are afraid of shipwrecks.

She wanted him to wear cow hide.

In the last rehearsal I decided to add a detail to the script, a missing detail about the way he got into the scene ... he stumbled in and staggered blind with excess, always laughing. This is the scene that made a strong impression on Nora. She was delighted, perhaps because she saw her mirror image, a simile, in the Libertador. While he rolled on the floor, at the gates of Lima, his many female soldiers began carving the walls with the inscription

"ΠΑΡΜΕΝΕΙΔΗΣ ΠΥΡΗΤΟΣ ΟΥΛΙΑΔΗΣ ΦΘΣΙΚΟΣ" *Yes, a Libertador wearing lipstick and dressing in cow hide broke into the scene.*

At the end, six soldiers should come back to Buenos Aires. The Libertador should not be not among them. You have to play punk music as a background, that is what the students begged me for.

Nora seemed pleased. At the end of that rehearsal she approached me to have a talk. While shouting at a girl who obstinately jumped on a desk, she told me that my days as a substitute teacher were over.... That afternoon I walked all the way from school back to the hotel. No, one should not reprove one's pedestrian fate.

I spent the whole weekend in my room. I packed my books and finished the rest of the translation. On Sunday, someone knocked at the door. It was Nora. She came in bringing some cookies. Better, she used the cookies as an excuse to talk about my work and its images. We made conversation for a while, and I finally showed her the dictionaries, the camera, the many versions of the poem.... I also gave her some ideas about how to finish the script.

Then Nora took my right hand kindly, and put an envelope on it. And in the envelope there were bills and coins. Enough money to leave by train from Bahía Blanca, and by ship from Buenos Aires.

ONTOLOGY

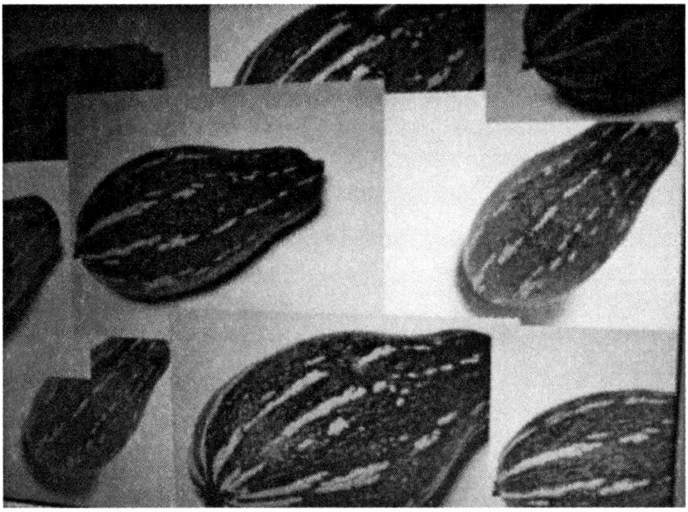

Merciless transformations, then, are to take place, and are taking place here and there, transformations of being that are carried out by themselves, beyond their limits, beyond any "natural" categorizing. There transformations are to take place in our own bodies as well. But is this uncertainty, this *κόρος,* completely alien to the pampas? Doesn't Borges's paragraph acknowledge this excess: "Like all men in Babylon I have been a proconsul; like all, a slave; I have also known omnipotence, opprobium jail" (Borges, *Ficciones,* 65)? How is ontology to be defined with regard to the well-known fact that "for one reasonable line or one straightforward note there are leagues of insensate cacophony, of verbal farragoes and incoherences" (*Ficciones,* 81)?

Aira has exemplified this *κόρος*, this becoming other in the figure of Rosas. The tyrant who orders dictionaries, the gaucho with blue eyes, the federalist who lives captive or secluded in Palermo, the ferocious Restaurer of Law, the one for whom only the allegorical is real. Again, Borges evinces this excess:

> Perhaps Rosas
> was only the implacable butcher our grandfathers thought him;
> I think of him now, like ourselves,
> as a creature of chance enclosed in an action's parentheses:
> he lived out the everyday anguish of things
> and for better or worse troubled
> the age's uncertainty. (Borges, *Selected Poems*, 11)

The pursuit of truth with regard to Rosas is also a pursuit of something that is already taking place, for truth is also in being, and in a way that being itself is fullfilled by truth, exceeded by truth. We can grasp this idea if we are acquainted with stillness, *ἡσυχία, siesta.*

Siesta offers itself to the hero as unconcealment, *κόρος*. It is a call for excess more than a prefiguration. The character of the hero, then, is manifested in certain excesses, in displaying a defiant, rather a bravado extravagance, as well as in the whimsical decisions, the visions, the other of mystical appearance that takes place, that fills the narrative in such a way that the continuum is no longer pursued, but manifested in an interpretation, in a (hi)story that already precludes, already unfolds the disclosedness of being in such a character. Quiroga, then, exceeds his being a *caudillo:* Sarmiento portrays him as rooted in the pampas, but also as being aware of the cycles to come. His visit to Buenos Aires is to remain obscure unless we acknowledge this cruelty, this excess. Further, Quiroga demands a coach with four horses to enter into death. He is wearing his purple *gala* uniform. Isn't this already an excess, futurism? (Cf. Marinetti, *The Futurist Cookbook*).

Such an interpretation of the hero is not due to a misunderstanding or a certain lack of historicality, for it is already grounded on the glimpses that Quiroga had in his *siesta,* a preliminary *siesta* before leading toward Barranca Yaco. There are, as in any murderous events, rumors unfolding what is to take place. Retelling is always foretelling. Rosas, the name, the image, the fashion, does not remain in the shadow. His actions are well known in advance for everyone, including Quiroga.

We mention fashion because aesthetics surrounds Quiroga throughout. It is not only his uniform, but also his hair with a style due the very morning of the murder, the silver knife in his *apero,* suede English boots, a *revenque* made in Buenos Aires. Truth, then, exceeds its temporal reality, its place in an assertion, to become fully manifest in any sign, in any gesture, in any motion. If this is the case, motion itself, then, is a sign of truth, its cloth, its fashion, and consequently the condition of excess and circulation. Borges, again, offers this excess:

> The coach swayed from side to side, creaking up the slope;
> a great bulk of a coach, voluminous, funereal.
> Four black horses with a tinge of death in their dark coats
> were drawing six souls in terror and one wide awake and bold.
> Alongside the postilions a black man was galloping.
> To ride to your death in a carriage—what a splendid thing to do! (*Selected Poems,* 35)

The search for the real in any description of Quiroga or Rosas remains fruitless unless we give up our temporal expectations of thinking of them as over or done with, and give place to the excess that these figures manifest. To say it differently, the reality of Rosas is to be thought of as manifested in the excess of the real. As Aira has posited it in *The Hare,* the question of the real concerns (i) whether entities that supposedly "transcend the narrative" (the captive, the hare, Repetido, the lost child) are taking place at all; (ii) whether the continuum can be adequately proved; and (iii) what the meaning of reality signifies in general in the pampas.

(i) The Duck's Egg. The Politics of Reality.

As a means of ensuring the continuum that is the pampas, that is reality itself, the story of "the duck's egg is the most effective of all" (*The Hare,* 120). For Clarke, whose view of the real, of the politics of reality, is a temporal one, Coliqueo can only appear as a promiscuous, lying, incoherent, misleading chieftain. What is at stake here is the question of what is to be admitted as "real." Coliqueo is misrepresented by temporality, his speech is seen as merely creating "monstrous sentences, joining the subject of one with the predicate of another, in order to increase their vagueness," when he is in fact addressing the politics of the real: what is real is excessive, *ἄπειρον*, displayed in *κόρος*. Cafulcurá tells stories whose meanings exceed mere (hi)storizing, or even any political purpose as such.

The political, indeed, is to be thought beyond the hygienic and the hocus-pocus, in terms of the excess that the stories offer as a continuum. These stories about twins, the hare, the blue gallstone, the duck's egg, make allusions to the real and constitute the ground for the political as such. Clarke believes that "the key element in that equilibrium, ... is Cafulcurá" (*The Hare*, 129), rather than an excessive reality. Stories are always more than stories, and unfold beings as we may never have considered them before. Thus, the story of the duck's egg manifests an object of study, and Clarke "would benefit from it" (*The Hare*, 131); but it also concerns everlasting peace. It is in this sense that Coliqueo is talking about "reality, tangible things, things that can be thought about without a sense of shame" (*The Hare*, 131). The reality of the duck's egg "lies elsewhere," in its excess of reality and purpose; that is what Coliqueo is asking Clarke, to "get that duck's egg for me. With all your knowledge, and with time at your disposal which I don't have because of all the problems I have to contend with here, and above all with a mind like yours free from prejudice, you will find it in no time. And then I'll be the true emperor" (*The Hare*, 132).

(ii) An Ontological Proof of the Continuum.

Aira has made explicit that any ontological inquiry is necessarily related to the question of the discontinuity of the territory, and that if one is to inquire about being, one needs to ask "where," "where is this continuum?" Clarke finds—immersed in the war of the hare—that "it was everywhere, including Cafulcurá's affirmation." The continuum postulated by Zeno and operating in the pampas is "a perfect *passe-partout*, an impalpable thread running through everything," a regress *ad infinitum* yet fully present. That is why "he could begin anywhere," even without making any effort. The hare displays this continuum in itself: "a good emblem for a strategic battle plan, because of its unexpected leaps, its elusive speed, its flexibility, the way it stared in fascination at the rising or setting sun (its indifference to whether it was sunrise or sunset mirrored the indifference as to victory or defeat that characterises a true fascination with war)" (*The Hare*, 197–198); but the hare moves to another element, anything: "The line. The horizon. The wanderer. The inversion of perspective. Everything else. And so on" (*The Hare*, 197–198).

Thus, to characterize the phenomenologically real—as Heidegger suggests—is to exceed the limits of any explicit existential-ontological basis. It may be experienced by means of emotion (Macedonio), the recollection of life cycles (Borges), or captivity (Aira). Reality exceeds resisting, or better, it offers itself: inexhaustibility (Ross), *ἄπειρον* (Zeno). If one is to work out these phenomena analytically, one is to do it beyond the limits imposed by temporality: Being is taking place* here and there, circulating, depreciating, coming-to-be and passing-away. "From that point on, Clarke began to understand something which reassured him completely with regard to simultaneity: it was subordinated to the narrative" (Aira, *The Hare*, 193).

Cruelty exceeds phenomenology because cruelty puts a demand on beings; that of doubling and being otherwise than themselves. This is what mintage, fashion, signs, and images make explicit, by putting into question the "within the pampas" posited by temporal ontology. This phenomenon has been already thematized in Western ontology from Zeno's notion of *ἄπειρον* to Kant's notion of the sublime, but it is to remain hidden until we move away from temporality, and posit the question of being as taking place here and there.

All the jokes that circulate after the default and paraphrase Borges's "Argumentum ornithologicum" (I close my eyes and I see the national debt. Is its number defined or undefined? This problem involves the existence of God [Cf. Borges, Dreamtigers, 29; Borges, *El Hacedor*, 165]) exceed the mere acknowledgment that such a debt constitutes a burden, or that beyond a certain limit it does not really matter, it is a cipher, because it is equally impossible to pay it back. These jokes ask for a continuum, or rather, for the real to unfold in forms that one may not evince, but are already there. There is, then, some kind of reversal, of inversion taking place in any reasoning with regard to reality. If reality is *ἄπειρον*, excessive, inexhaustible, then one has to ask why some events are not taking place in the pampas. But then one has to go back to that which the Greek thematized in terms such as motion and stillness, or even mimesis; or ultimately, thematize the paradox of the captive, and the events of New Rome as epiphanies of something that must take place.

(iii) The Question of Laughter.

"Reality" is defined by what is taking place and exceeding its place.* This definition does not belong only to the pampas but has been manifest in Western ontology all along. Indeed, this definition makes problematic the relation between language and reality. One may say, for instance, that reality exceeds language. Such an assertion, as Ross points out in *The Limits of Language,* only says that reality is inexhaustible, but it frequently hides the fact that language itself is inexhaustible, and that language itself steps out of itself. We have thematized this ontological difficulty with regard to signs and assertions, insisting that validity goes beyond what is *in* an assertion. Validity exceeds any assertion. Parmenides' poem and the events of New Rome manifest that the real is taking place and exceeding its place in images. Furthermore, Pausanias—who problematized the question of being in terms of "where"—reports that the real depicted by images terrifies men; and it is not until they are seated in the chair of memory and recollect truth that they come to laugh again. The real is to be conceived by phenomena that we have not problematized in our analysis, and which may require further enquiry. Laughter displays reality "at the expense of the body" (Bergson, *Laughter,* 29), and demands a certain expansion—rather, extension—to take place in such a way that what is asserted with regard to the real exceeds the mere ready-at-hand or present-at-hand of beings. Borges has also observed this with regard to the gaucho's use of irony, but our suggestion goes beyond any analytic of *Dasein* in the pampas. The question of being in the pampas is an ontological one, and demands an answer that cannot be less than hyperinflated, *ἄπειρον,* squashed.

NOTES

Page

2.* In Macedonio Fernández's and Parmenides's thematizing of being, *siesta*, *ἡσυχία* is a necessary step in order to give laws in the pampas. Yet, can we still think of photography as the activity of the *κουροτροφος*? (Cf. Kingsley, *In the Dark Places of Wisdom;* West, *The Orphic Hymns*).

2.** Aristotle and Saussure have bound alteration to the notions of before and after. *Vicinity* is a notion highly neglected in Aristotle's treatment of the Eleatic philosophers (Cf. Aristotle, *Physics*, I, 187a12–189b30).

3.* Olivieri's cussing the troops, who refused to follow *ἡσυχία*, and replaced truth with mintage as the primordial concern in the pampas.

3.** Cf. Einsenstein, S. "The Cinematographic Principle and the Ideogram," In Braudy and Cohen, eds. *Film Theory and Criticism*, 127–138. Doxography has separated these from the biographies. Kirk and Raven call these "apocryphal biographical tales" (Cf. *The Presocratic Philosophers*, 321).

4.* "So long as the *mise en scène* remains, even in the minds of the boldest director, a simple means of presentation, an accessory mode of expressing the work ... with no significance of its own...." (Artaud, *The Theatre and Its Double*, 105).

4.** (Cf. Echeverría, E. *La Cautiva*). Echeverría's aesthetics is yet to be understood beyond the temporal frame of civilization and barbarism. (Cf. Echeverría, E. *La Cautiva*). *La Cautiva*, indeed, offers the resoluteness that Deleuze & Guattari's treatise on nomadology demands (Cf. Deleuze & Guattari, *A Thousand Plateaus*, 351–423).

5.* "a branch of fictional literature ..." Borges writes in *Tlön, Uqbar, Orbis Tertius*, "the fact that any philosophical system is bound in advance to be a dialectical game, a *Philosophie des Als Ob*, means that systems abound, unbelievable systems, beautifully constructed or else sensational in effect. The metaphysicians of Tlön are not looking for truth, not even for an approximation of it; they after a kind of amazement. They consider metaphysics a branch of fantastic literature" (Borges, *Ficciones*, 25).

7.* It is also said that Darwin himself felt victim of it twice.... "Prilidiano did not insist, because his gadfly mind had already gone into reverse. However absurd the idea about some animals being descended from others might be, it had given him a notion as to how he might resolve the dilemma of his painting of Facunda taking her siesta. Which at the very last was proof that some ideas can descend from others" (Aira, *The Hare*, 19).

9.* (Cf. Aristotle, *Physics*, VI, 239b30). Note that *κρόνος* is an addendum, an excessive way of solving Zeno's paradox.

17.* Who can not claim to be *Dasein*? "I who longed to be someone else, to weigh / judgments, to read books, to hand down the law, / will lie in the open out in these swamps; / but a secret joy somehow swells my breast. / I see at last that I am face to face with my South American destiny...." (Borges, *Selected Poems 1923–1967*, 83).

22.* For a summary of Parmenides journey into the underworld (Cf. Pausanias, *Description of Greece*, II, 348–355).

29.* Carriego interrogates.... See Borges's remarks on humor as essential to friendship (Borges, *Evaristo Carriego*, 97).

38.* ... about the right of inspection, and its labyrinthine aspects (Cf. Derrida, *Right of Inspection*, 8–12).

42.* Sarmiento and Martínez Estrada needed a philosophy of "characters."... (Cf. Hernández, *The Gaucho Martín Fierro*, 1325).

46.* When Heidegger asks after the frame he is already leaving room for fashion ... (Cf. Heidegger, "The Question Concerning Technology." In Heidegger, *Basic Writings*, 325–327).

59.* Kant's notion of the sublime ... (Cf. Kant, *Critique of Judgment*, 97–125; Artaud, "On the Balinese Theatre." *The Theatre and Its Double*, 53–67).

73.* About this closeness to non-being (Cf. Fernández, *Selected Writings in Translation*, 25–27).

137.* ... the excess was followed by monstruous cycles of depreciation. These lines from the *Martín Fierro* contain this idea, "I've earned my living by my work / ever since I was a child, / and though I was always at the bottom / and don't know what it means to rise high—we can get tired out as well / by too much suffering, curse it! (Hernández, *Martín Fierro*, 975).

141.* Production, *ποιήσις*, ambition, the ever lasting peace.... "We have signed a treaty of everlasting peace. It's a dead letter, but I'm happy enough with it. My concern is my people: production, development, foreign affairs. Within my modest domain, I aim to be a model stateman" (Aira, *The Hare,* 127).

147.* ... [they] come to forget that recession was already taking place in the pampas (Cf. Aira, *The Hare,* 20–21).

148.* A Chinese Novel.... (Cf. Aira, *Una Novela China*).

154.* "A public that shudders at train wrecks, that is familiar with earthquakes, plagues, revolutions, wars; that is sensitive to the disordered anguish of love. ..." (Artaud, *The Theatre and Its Double,* 75).

179.* Being is taking place.... (Cf. Aira, *The Hare,* 182–203).

180.* *Reality* is defined.... "That's just it, we don't live on the surface" (Aira, *The Hare,* 152–170).

REFERENCES

The Collected Dialogues of Plato. Edith Hamilton and Huntington Cairns, eds. Princeton: Princeton University Press, 1989.

Aeschylus. *Agamemnon.* Trans. Herbert Weir Smyth. Cambridge, MA: Harvard University Press.

Aira, Cesar. *Copi.* Rosario: Beatriz Viterbo, 1984.

———. *Ema, la Cautiva.* Rosario: Beatriz Viterbo, 1996.

———. *The Hare.* London: Serpent's Tail, 1998.

———. *Una Novela China.* Rosario: Beatriz Viterbo, 1986.

Aquinas, T. *Summa Theological.* Cambridge: Blackfriars; New York: McGraw-Hill, 1964.

Aristotle. *On Coming-to-be and Passing-away.* Trans. E. S. Furley. Cambridge, MA: Harvard University Press, 1955.

———. *On Interpretation.* Trans. Hugh Tredennick. Cambridge, MA: Harvard University Press, 1962.

———. *The Metaphysics.* Trans. Hugh Tredennick. Vol. 1. Cambridge, MA: Harvard University Press, 1947.

———. *The Metaphysics.* Trans. Hugh Tredennick. Vol. 2. Cambridge, MA: Harvard University Press, 1947.

———. *The Physics.* Trans. Philip H. Wicksteed and Francis M. Cornford. Vol. 1. Cambridge, MA: Harvard University Press, 1970.

———. *The Physics.* Trans. Philip H. Wicksteed and Francis M. Cornford. Vol. 2. Cambridge, MA: Harvard University Press, 1952.

———. *The Poetics.* Trans. W. Hamilton Fyfe. Cambridge, MA: Harvard University Press, 1953.

Artaud, Antonin. *Ouvres Completes.* Paris: Gallimard, 1978.

———. *The Theatre and Its Double.* New York: Grove Press, 1958.

Augustine, St. *The City of God.* Trans. Marcus Dods. New York: The Modern Library, 1950.

Benjamin, Walter. *Illuminations.* New York: Schocken Books, 1968.

Bergson, Henry. *Laughter.* Trans. Cloudesley Brereton and Fred Rothwell. London: MacMillan and Co., 1913.

Berkeley, G. A. *A Treatise Concerning the Principles of Human Knowledge.* New York: The Bobbs-Merrill Co., 1957.

Blanchot, Maurice. *The Space of Literature.* Lincoln: University of Nebraska Press, 1984.

Borges, Jorge Luis. *The Aleph and Other Stories 1933–1969*. Trans. Norman Thomas di Giovanni. New York: E. P. Dutton & Co., 1970.
———. *Collected Fictions*. Trans. Andrew Hurley. New York: Viking, 1998.
———. *Dreamtigers*. Trans. Mildred Boyerl and Harold Morland. Austin, TX: University of Texas Press, 1964.
———. *Evaristo Carriego*. Trans. Norman Thomas di Giovanni. New York: E. P. Dutton & Co., 1984.
———. *Ficciones*. New York: Grove Press, 1962.
———. *In Praise of Darkness*. Trans. Norman Thomas di Giovanni. New York: E. P. Dutton & Co., 1974.
———. *Obras Completas*. Buenos Aires: Emecé Editores, 1994.
———. *Other Inquisitions 1937–1952*. Trans. Ruth L. C. Simms. Austin, TX: University of Texas Press, 1964.
———. *Selected Non-Fictions*. Trans. Esther Allen, Suzanne Jill Levine, and Eliot Weinberger. New York: Viking, 1999.
———. *Selected Poems 1923–1967*. Edited by Norman Thomas di Giovanni. New York: Delacorte Press—Seymour Lawrence, 1972.
Eisenstein, Sergei. "The Cinematographic Principle and the Ideogram." In Braudy, L. and M. Cohen, eds. *Film Theory and Criticism*. New York, Oxford: Oxford University Press, 1999, 127–38.
Breton. Andre. *Manifestes du Surréalisme*. Paris: Gallimard, 1979.
Chantraine, Pierre. *Dictionnaire Étymologique de la Langue Grecque*. Paris: Editions Klincksieck, 1968.
Clement of Alexandria. *Miscellanies*. Leipzig, 1905.
Corominas, J. *Diccionario Etimológico de la Lengua Castellana*. Madrid: Gredos, 1954.
Cordero, N.-L. *Les Deux Chemins de Parménide*. Paris: Libraire J. Vrin, 1984.
Coloubaritsis, L. *Mythe et Philosophie chez Parménide*. Paris: Editions Ousia, S. C., 1986.
Craik, J. *The Face of Fashion*. London: Routledge, 1994.
Crespi Valls, A. *Primer Centenario de la Legión Agrícola Militar*. Bahía Blanca: Panzini Hermanos S. R. L., 1956.
Deleuze, Gilles, and Felix Guattari. *Anti-Oedipus: Capitalism and Schizophrenia*. Minneapolis: University of Minnesota Press, 1998.
———. *A Thousand Plateaus: Capitalism* and *Schizophrenia*. Minneapolis and London: University of Minnesota Press, 1996.
Derrida, J. *De la Grammatologie*. Paris: Editions de Minuit, 1967.
———. *Disseminations*. Chicago: The University of Chicago Press, 1981.
———. *Given Time: 1. Counterfait Money*. Chicago and London: The University of Chicago Press, 1992.
———. *Margins of Philosophy*. Chicago: University of Chicago Press, 1982.
———. *Of Grammatology*. Baltimore and London: The Johns Hopkins University Press, 1997.
———. *Right of Inspection*. New York: The Monacelli Press, 1985.
Diels, H. and W. Kranz. *Die Fragmente der Vorsokratiker*. Berlin: Weidmannsche Verlagbuchhandlung, 1960.

———. *Die Fragmente der Vorsokratiker.* Vol. 1. Berlin: Weidmannsche Verlagbuchhandlung, 1961.
Diogenes Laertius, *Life of Eminent Philosophers.* Trans. R. D. Hicks. Vol. 2. Cambridge, MA: Harvard University Press, 1950.
Dodds, E. R. *The Greeks and the Irrational.* Berkeley and Los Angeles: University of California Press, 1956.
Docphie, A. "À Propos de Koros dans l'Agammenon d'Eschyle: Mise au Point Préliminaire." *Recherches de Philologie et de Linguistique.* (1968): 125–38.
Durkheim, Emile. *Le Suicide.* Paris: PUF, 1960.
Echeverría, Esteban. *La Cautiva; El Matadero.* Buenos Aires: Peuser, 1958.
Eliade, Mircea. *Shamanism.* London: Routledge & Kegan Paul, 1964.
Empedocles. *Empedocles: The Extant Fragments.* M. R. Wright ed., New Haven and London: Yale University Press, 1981.
The Poem of Empedocles. Trans. Brad Inwood. Toronto: University of Toronto Press, 1992.
Engelbert, J. A. *Macedonio Fernández and the Spanish American New Novel.* New York: State University of New York Press, 1978.
———. *Macedonio: Selected Writings in Translation.* Fort Worth: Latitude Press, 1984.
Fernandez, Macedonio. *Museo de la Novela de la Eterna.* Buenos Aires: Centro Editor de América Latina, 1967.
———. *Papeles de Recienvenido, y Continuación de la Nada.* Buenos Aires: Corregidor, 1989.
Fontanella de Weinberg, M. B. *Aspectos del Español Hablado en el Río de la Plata durante los Siglos XVI y XVII.* Bahía Blanca: Universidad Nacional del Sur, 1982.
Foucault, Michel. *Madness and Civilization.* New York: Random House, Inc., 1965.
———. *The Order of Things.* New York: Vintage Books, 1970.
Griffin, Susan. *Women and Nature.* New York: Sierra Club Books, 2000.
Godel, R. *Les Sources Manuscrites du Cours de Linguistique Générale de F. de Saussure.* Genéve: H. Studer, S. A., 1957.
Harl, M. "Recherches sur l'origenisme de Origene: la'Satiéte (*Koros*) de la Contemplation comme Motif de la Chute des Âmes." *Studia Patristica,* 8 (1966): 373–405.
Hegel, G. W. F. *Lectures on the Philosophy of World History.* Trans. H. B. Nisbet. Cambridge: Cambridge University Press, 1975.
Heidegger, M. *An Introduction to Metaphysics.* New Haven and London: Yale University Press, 1987.
———. *Being and Time.* Trans. John Macquarrie and Edward Robinson. New York: Harper San Francisco, 1962.
———. *Existence and Being.* London: Vision, 1949.
———. *Parmenides.* Bloomington and Indianapolis: Indiana University Press, 1992.

Hernandez, J. *The Gaucho Martín Fierro.* Trans. C. E. Ward. New York: State University of New York Press, 1967.

Herbst, R. *Dictionary of Commercial, Financial, and Legal Terms.* Zug, Switzerland: Translegal Ltd. Vol. III, 1986.

Hesiod. *Works and Days, and Theogony.* Indianapolis and Cambridge: Hackett Publishing Co., 1993.

Homer. *The Iliad.* Trans. A. T. Murray. Cambridge, MA: Harvard University Press, 1947.

———. *The Odyssey.* Cambridge, MA: Harvard University Press, 1995.

Hudson, G. H. *The Purple Land.* New York: The Modern Library, 1927.

———. *Tales of the Pampas.* New York: Alfred A. Knopf, 1916.

Kant, I. *Critique of Judgment.* Trans. J. H. Bernard. New York: Hafner Press, 1951.

———. *Kritik Der Urteilskraft.* In *Immanuel Kants Werke.* Ed. Dr. Benzion Kellermann. Vol. 5. Berlin: Verlag Bei Bruno Cassirer, 1914.

Kingsley, Peter. *In the Dark Places of Wisdom.* Inverness, CA: The Golden Sufi Center, 1999.

Kirk, G. S. and J. E. Raven, *The Presocratic Philosophers.* Cambridge: Cambridge University Press, 1962.

Kusch, Rodolfo. *Obras Completas.* Vol. 1. Rosario: Editorial Fundacion Ross, 1998.

———. *Obras Completas.* Vol. 2. Rosario: Editorial Fundacion Ross, 1999.

Levinas, Emmanuel. *Totality and Infinity.* Pittsburgh: Duquesne University Press, 1969.

Liddell, H. G. and R. Scott. *A Greek-English Lexicon.* Oxford: Clarendon Press, 1996.

Lingis, A. *The Imperative.* Bloomington and Indianapolis: Indiana University Press, 1998.

Long, A. A. and D. N. Sedley. *The Hellenistic Philosophers.* Cambridge: Cambridge University Press, 1987.

MacKirahan Jr., R. "Zeno." In Long, A. A. ed. *Early Greek Philosophy.* Cambridge: Cambridge University Press, 1999.

Marinetti, F. T. *The Futurist Cookbook.* Trans. Suzanne Brill. San Francisco: Bedford Arts, Publishers, 1989.

Martínez Estrada, Ezequiel. *Radiografía de la Pampa.* Buenos Aires: Losada, 1961.

———. *X-Ray of the Pampas.* Austin, TX: University of Texas Press, 1971.

Meijier, P. A. *Parmenides Beyond the Gates.* Amsterdam: J. C. Gieben Publisher, 1997.

Mourelatos, Alexander. *The Route of Parmenides.* New Haven and London: Yale University Press, 1970.

Nagy, Gregory. *Pindar's Homer: The Lyric Possession of an Epic Past.* Baltimore: John Hopkins Press, 1990.

Pareto, V. *Manuel d'Économie Politique.* Paris: Marcel Giard, 1927.

Parmenides. *Fragments. A Text and Translation with an Introduction by David Gallop.* Trans. David Gallop. Toronto: Toronto University Press, 1984.

Pausanias. *Description of Greece.* Cambridge, MA: Harvard University Press, 1961.
Pindar. *The Odes of Pindar.* Trans. Sir John Sandys. Cambridge, MA: Harvard University Press, 1946.
Plato. *Cratylus.* Trans. Harold N. Fowler. Cambridge, MA: Harvard University Press, 1996.
———. *Parmenides.* Trans. Harold N. Fowler. Cambridge, MA: Harvard University Press, 1996.
———. *Phaedo.* Trans. Harold N. Fowler. Cambridge, MA: Harvard University Press, 1960.
———. *Republic.* Trans. Paul Shorey. Cambridge, MA: Harvard University Press, 1970.
———. *Sophist.* Trans. Harold N. Fowler. Cambridge, MA: Harvard University Press, 1952.
———. *Symposium.* Trans. W. R. M. Lamb. Cambridge, MA: Harvard University Press, 1946.
Pliny. *Natural History.* Cambridge, MA: Harvard University Press, 1947.
Ross, Stephen David. *The Gift of Beauty.* Albany: State University of New York Press, 1996.
———. *The Gift of Touch.* Albany: State University of New York Press, 1998.
———. *The Limits of Language.* New York: Fordham University Press, 1994.
Saussure, F. de. *Cours de Linguistique Générale.* Paris: Payot, 1949.
———. Course in General Linguistics. New York: McGraw-Hill, 1966.
Sarmiento, Domingo F. *Facundo.* Madrid: Editora Nacional, 1975.
Seidel, M. *Martin Heidegger and the Presocratics.* Lincoln: University of Nebraska Press, 1964.
Simplicius. *Corollaries on Place and Time.* Trans. J. O. Urmson. Ithaca, NY: Cornell University Press, 1992.
———. *On Aristotle's Physics.* Trans. J. O. Urmson. Ithaca, NY: Cornell University Press, 1993.
Sontag, Susan. *On Photography.* New York: Anchor Books, 1989.
Suárez, Francisco. *Disputationes Metaphysicae.* Hildesheim: G. Olms, 1965.
Tarán, Luis. *Parmenides.* Princeton: Princeton University Press, 1965.
Trendall, A. D. *Red Figure Vases of South Italy and Sicily.* London: Thames and Hudson, 1989.
West, D. *Some Cults of Greek Goddesses and Female Daemons of Oriental Origin.* Verlag Butzon & Bercker Kevelaer, 1995.
West, M. L. *The Orphic Poems.* Oxford: Clarendon Press, 1983.
———. *Theogony.* Oxford: Clarendon Press, 1966.
Wittig, Monique. *The Lesbian Body.* Boston: Beacon Press, 1973.
Zuntz, G. *Persephone.* Oxford: Clarendon Press, 1971.